CHRISTIANITY
INCORPORATED

CHRISTIANITY INCORPORATED

How Big Business Is Buying the Church

Michael L. Budde &
Robert W. Brimlow

Brazos Press

A Division of Baker Book House Co
Grand Rapids, Michigan 49516

Published by Brazos Press
a division of Baker Book House Company
P.O. Box 6287, Grand Rapids, MI 49516-6287

Printed in the United States of America

For current information about all releases from Brazos Press, visit our web site:
http://www.brazospress.com

Contents

Introduction

Anybody with an ounce of common sense knows to stay away from the topics of religion, sex, or business in polite company. Not only does everybody think they're an expert on all three subjects, people usually get annoyed when somebody else paints a different picture than the one most folks prefer.

We've been told, by family members and colleagues alike, that *combined* we still fall short of the proverbial ounce of common sense. In fact, it may well be that there really are no strangers in the world—only people we haven't yet alienated. It isn't that we go out of our way to make people uncomfortable, but that often seems to happen whenever our work invites the gospel to critique everyday lives and loyalties. The gospel makes *us* uncomfortable as well, so why shouldn't we share that discomfort—which is good news, although of a rather peculiar sort—with people curious and brave enough to lift a book entitled *Christianity Incorporated?*

You won't find a lot of sex in this book, but you will find what we hope is a gospel- and church-centered analysis of how Christianity and capitalism are shaping one another these days. "Shaping" may be too tame a word for much of what's going on, in fact. At times it looks more like institutional cross-dressing, in which churches and big corporations can't wait to run around in each other's clothes, each trying to pass for the other.

Some of what this role-swapping produces is amusing, some of it is interesting, and some of it is just plain silly. But most of what

7

it is looks like a bad deal for churches trying to be distinctive communities loyal to Jesus' Way in the world. Corporations may well see Christianity as another resource to be used and discarded— in the workplace, in advertising, even at the hour of our death— but Christianity shouldn't be so naive to think that churches can imitate the corporate giants without risking some essentials of their faith and mission. Not only that, when Christianity lends its stories, symbols, and integrity to the corporate world, it always gets them back in need of some serious dry cleaning and repairs.

For all the troubling trends and shallow thinking that have led the churches into their present predicament, things are not entirely hopeless. When churches start to worry more about discipleship than market share, when they stop trying to soothe the consciences of political and economic powers, then they'll be on their way toward creating Christian communities that won't be confused with Microsoft, Disney, or Exxon. When churches start to get comfortable wearing the armor of Christ rather than the Armani suits of corporate boardrooms, the cross-dressing of Christianity Incorporated will itself be seen as offensive and impolite— which lets people like us off the hook, with or without that ounce of common sense we've been lacking for so long.

1

Being Useful in the Global Age

limpses of the future sometimes appear in pretty unpredictable places. We've seen the future of Christianity in the United States in a journal called the *Armed Forces Comptroller.*

Calling this periodical obscure is to commit criminal understatement. Its focus on accounting, budgeting, and resource management in the military ensures that most people will live and die never knowing of its existence—much less ever having read it. Yet in its winter 1997 issue, an article by James W. Daniels Jr. provides a realistic—and to us, troubling—picture of the present and future status of Christianity in our society.

In "The Command Master Religious Plan—A Cost Model for Chaplain Activities in the United States Army," Daniels describes a new resource management philosophy (with relevant software) designed to give army budgeting personnel precise information on the requirements, cost, and expenditures related to military chaplaincy. The article itself is steeped in an unholy marriage of military bureaucrat-ese, management jargon, and auditor-speak. What comes through loud and clear, however, is an utterly pragmatic, what's-in-it-for-me view of religion.

Forget churches and synagogues as autonomous communities with their own sense of purpose and mission—in the army, they are just another part of the infrastructure, necessary for smooth and efficient operations. The army now manages religion under a Command Master Religious Plan (CMRP), with eleven "Religious Support Areas" (RSA), including pastoral care, religious education, and religious services, comprising the "business area" of military chaplaincy. Under the CMRP, a base commander will be able to identify the "cost" of every "unit" of "religious service"—every worship, prayer service, Catholic Mass—provided to "customers" using that RSA. A commander can then look for areas of potential cost savings via activities that can be "simplified" or "performed more efficiently." While Daniels's article does not directly deal with questions of "outcomes assessment" or "quality of output," other parts of the military's managerial process have methods for ensuring that "military religious support" pays acceptable dividends in terms of troop morale, efficiency, enthusiasm, and peace of mind.

Beneath the comptroller's jargon, one can see a set of assumptions regarding the proper role of the church in capitalist democracies such as the United States. These assumptions, we suggest, are shared by nearly all powerful political and economic institutions, labels of political "liberal" and "conservative" notwithstanding. Foremost among them is the notion that Christianity must be "useful" in order to be a legitimate player in our contemporary world. It must help people perform their duties as defined by the secular *status quo,* not from within ecclesial traditions unless the two are identical. In addition to enabling people to work within the existing order more efficiently, Christianity must also boost people emotionally and psychologically during stressful times, and must enable them to be good citizens, employees, consumers, patriots, and family members. Indeed, for Christianity to be relevant today, it must do for the whole of society what chaplains do in the armed forces—meet spiritual needs and personal crises, provide legitimation and explanation for the way things are, and generate loyalties to the collective and its purposes.

Chaplaincy has a long and rich legacy in Christian history. While we think that military chaplaincies are indefensible compromises of Jesus' proclamation of the kingdom of God, we nonetheless respect the comfort and assistance chaplains have provided to soldiers and their families. In other institutional contexts such as hospitals and colleges, chaplains pray with and for patients, families, and students in crisis; they provide an array of important services and supports to persons in stressful situations. As one manifestation of the Christian imperative to serve one's fellows, the activities that chaplains perform have been an important part of the ministry of the churches.

Chaplaincy—in the military or the capitalist firm, for example—requires churches to situate themselves within the belly of such powerful institutions while still attempting to preserve their ecclesial independence. For chaplaincy to be a defensible Christian practice, churches must be able to operate within rules, structures, norms, and practices created by non-Christian powers in ways that do not compromise the churches' fidelity to the gospel or a christocentric view of reality (a near-impossible move in most cases, we suggest). Unless the churches retain their distinctiveness and autonomy in such contexts, most forms of chaplaincy risk becoming absorbed and co-opted for ends other than seeking and witnessing to the kingdom of God.

Yet it is this distinctiveness, autonomy, and gospel-centered orientation that the church's agents all too often sacrifice when entering chaplaincy relations with structures of economic and political power. In order for chaplains to understand, serve, and empathize with persons who lead and serve such powerful institutions, chaplains must themselves submit to the formative processes (physical, emotional, affective, and spiritual) of the institutions. Hence business chaplains must have corporate training or education, and must internalize a capitalist worldview; military chaplains must experience military formation ("basic training" and more advanced processes) and adopt the worldview of peace through strength, service through death-dealing, and national self-preservation as the ultimate goal.

The assumption that such intensive formation leaves the gospel untouched seems entirely insupportable. Instead, in deciding to serve the "principalities and powers" (Eph. 3:10 RSV) on their own turf, the gospel becomes trimmed to conform to the requisites of these principalities and powers. The mere appearance of ecclesial independence, as in military chaplaincy, substitutes for substantive independence. For example, within the U.S. military, chaplains are unarmed in accord with an old Christian intuition that representatives of Christ should not be killers (an intuition ignored during the Crusades and other ignoble eras in church history). The chaplain's aide, however, *must* be armed and perform all the duties (including killing) of a combat participant; furthermore, chaplains themselves may assume a combatant's role *in extremis*. Additionally, the chaplains assigned to specialized units (like Rangers, psychological operations, and elite invasion forces) must undergo much of the same advanced training and indoctrination required of the soldiers they serve. Enabling persons to perform the tasks required of some special forces units—including assassinations, killing of unarmed civilians, torture, and the like (see Klare and Kornbluh, 1987) involves moral and psychological condition drastically at odds with Christian imperatives to love one's enemies and repay evil with good. One cannot accept such military norms and practices without simultaneously eviscerating, diluting, or redefining into inoffensiveness the life and message of Jesus as a source of Christian life and ethics (on the intensive conditioning required to turn people into killers, see for example Grossman, 1995). What is obvious in the case of military chaplaincy—that the gospel is compromised in becoming useful to a powerful institution—is also true via different processes when discussing other sorts of chaplaincy arrangements in capitalist democracies.

In this book, we give evidence of a broader blanket of chaplaincy descending over the church, one that reaches far beyond the blessing of military and state that has haunted the church since its formal accommodation to the Roman Empire in the fourth century. And while the subordination of the gospel to political power is at least capable of generating *debate* within the church—even after these centuries of compromised Christianity—the more recent captivity is not even recognized as such by most sectors of the Christian community. Whatever the merits of chaplaincy in specific or limited contexts, as an overall framework for Christians in society it is a theological monstrosity. It prostitutes the gospel, castrates the concept of discipleship, and reduces the church to the level of the Rotary Club or the Moose Lodge. It is unscriptural, contrary to the life and practice of Jesus, and a betrayal of the subversive nature of Christianity.

In suggesting that chaplaincy is an important category through which to examine contemporary questions of church and society, one must inevitably confront the near-total embrace of capitalism by the mainstream of Christianity in the United States and many other countries. While the theological legitimation of capitalism has a long history in most expressions of American Protestantism, it is a relatively new development of some importance in the Catholic Church. After centuries of opposition, arms-length relations, and suspicion between the Catholic Church and capitalism, the papacy of John Paul II has made its peace with capitalism—much to the delight of the middle-class churches in the United States and elsewhere. While Catholic leadership maintains that theirs is a "conditional" endorsement of capitalism—contingent upon a variety of social protections and policies—in practice that endorsement has been anything but conditional. No matter what outrages are perpetrated in the name of neoliberal reform or deregulation, neither the pope nor the American leaders of the Catholic Church will question the fundamentals of the economic order. Rather, they have accepted the roles of providing care for capitalism's casualties, moral support for its functionaries, spiritual solace to its rulers, and in-house whispers for "compassion"—chaplaincy, in other words.

As chaplain to capitalism, the church is besieged by needs on all sides. The current era of capitalism means greater emphasis on productivity, which translates into more demands made on fewer employees, who in turn must become more, not less, devoted to "their" firm. Firms must cultivate bonds of affection, common purpose, and mutual support between themselves and employees—no easy task, given the alienation and distrust among employees produced by wave after wave of corporate downsizing, layoffs, and movement toward temporary, part-time (and underpaid) employees. All of which inclines toward corporations seeking to provide a sense of "vocation" and "spiritual fulfillment" among the ranks of their employees, thus making secularized religious concepts (and some church programs) part of the corporate human resources arsenal.

This "meaning deficit" (a lack of internalized belief in the transcendent nature of one's life or vocation) affects people not simply as producers in capitalist society but also as consumers. A consequence of the relentless bombardment of marketing appeals, logos, and pitches (the average American experiences nearly sixteen thousand such encounters *per day*) is a dissatisfaction with materialism and consumerism. This discontentment is real but shallow—most people recognize the need to fill the emptiness produced by the search for the perfect basketball shoe, but they shy away from anything that might require sacrifice, self-denial, or a break with the basic premises of consumerist/capitalist ideology.

Churches help people with this disaffection by offering moralistic criticisms of consumerism (the speeches and documents of the pope are full of such attacks). If people would be less materialistic, say many church leaders, they would be happier and society would be better off. Thus, we receive annual Christmas messages from church leaders pleading that people focus on the "true meaning of Christmas" without any consideration of how utterly essential consumerism is to the functioning of contemporary capitalism. Without the willingness of people to buy, spend, and borrow for an unceasing supply of goods, novelties, and services, the modern market economy would grind to a halt. Consumerism and capitalism are so inseparable that society would be better off, according to business columnist Leonard Peikoff, if Americans were to "take the Christ out of Christmas, and turn the holiday into a guiltlessly egoistic, pro-reason, this-worldly, commercial celebration" (Peikoff, 1997).

Being a caretaker for capitalism requires that Christianity concern itself with more than economic questions, for capitalism has always been more than just a means of organizing economic processes. For example, the profound social and economic dislocation that capitalism causes worldwide also produces political fragmentation, diminished state capacities, and a rise of ethnic, separatist, and localist groups attacking the prerogatives and primacy of the nation-state. While these trends are more violently visible in other parts of the world (think of the former Yugoslavia, Rwanda, Mexico, and elsewhere), they produce anxiety among elites in the wealthy countries as well. With capitalism rendering

whole segments of American society economically unnecessary—
African-American men, for example—politicians and opinion
leaders worry about the "dis-uniting of America," the collapse of
"public spiritedness," and the decline of civic virtue as manifested
in voting and support for elected officials. Religious communities
in general—and Catholics in particular, under the banner of the
"Catholic Moment," a 1980s call for Catholics to revitalize the
moral underpinnings of the "American experiment"—are called
to rejuvenate the categories of citizenship and patriotism. The old
religious nationalism of white Protestantism is dead; a new expression, which merges civic duties and religious loyalties, is needed
if the United States is to avoid the descent into anarchy visible in
other parts of the world.

Civil Religion and Transnational Capitalism

How to understand patriotism, civic virtue, and religiosity in
global capitalism invites an examination of the usefulness (or lack
thereof) of a category in social analysis whose fortunes have risen
and fallen over the last half-century. That concept is civil religion,
and we believe that it remains a useful tool in exploring what it
might mean to be "church" in our time and place.

While civil religion has admitted of many competing defini-
tions and descriptions, the explanation offered by historian Robert
Linder (1996) is an adequate general formula:

> The widely but informally held set of fundamental principles con-
> cerning the history and destiny of a state or nation that help to
> bind that state or nation together. It is a collection of beliefs, val-
> ues, ceremonies, and symbols that gives sacred meaning to the
> political life of the community, provides the nation with an over-
> arching sense of unity that transcends all internal conflicts and dif-
> ferences, and relates the society to the realm of ultimate meaning.

Standard narratives of mainstream civil religion in the United
States are flavored with distinctively Protestant republican and biblical symbols and stories (the city on the hill, the New Jerusalem,

the new chosen people). This sort of civil religion ran aground during the 1960s, according to standard accounts, as its inability to account for the experiences of society's excluded—minority groups, women, dissenters, and the like—overwhelmed its ability to provide a vaguely Christian gloss to love of country and worship of what Will Herberg in 1955 described as the true object of mainstream American religion—namely, the "American Way of Life." It became incapable of providing the sort of religiously grounded legitimation most useful to powerholders—sufficient, in the words of Voltaire, to keep the servants from stealing the silver, but not the type likely to encourage religious practices and norms at odds with capitalism, patriotism, or the essentials of the system as presently constituted.

A little-explored facet of the decline of so-called traditional or mainline civil religion concerns the inability of churches to "deliver the goods" in terms of what has been called religious formation— that is, the capacity to shape people's attitudes, desires, and dispositions with the stories, symbols, and songs of the Christian tradition. Indeed, having stressed the continuities between being a good Christian and a good American for so long, many churches deemphasized those ecclesial practices that marked and constructed the distinctiveness of being Christian.

With a lag, such a crisis of formation describes the situation of contemporary U.S. Catholicism as well. Whatever uneven and selective formation was delivered by the system of Catholic enclaves and institutions of the pre-Vatican II era was in large measure neglected as most white Catholics moved firmly into the American middle class.

Another set of concerns omitted from standard sociological discussions of civil religion relate more directly to the concept of globalization. The late 1960s and early 70s marked the beginning, according to many economists, of the intensified transnationalization of production, finance, and commerce that comprise economic globalization: this emerged, in part, from the creation of a system of floating currency exchange rates and a worldwide move by business leaders toward economic deregulation and privatization. Changes in the flow and direction of human migration, enhanced cultural interaction, the changing patterns of engagement between sovereign states and transnational firms, and other factors recast many of the traditional problems faced by political and economic elites (and added a few new ones) that together have impelled a search for a new sort of functional civil religion in the early twenty-first century.

For example, we are persuaded that however it has varied, the modern state as an institutional form requires people in sufficient numbers willing to do three basic things: kill for it, die for it, and pay for it. From Costa Rica to Colombia, the United States to China, all modern states presuppose lethality on their behalf as a minimal requisite for statehood. How to secure loyalty, allegiance, and commitment sufficient to produce enough people willing to do these things—kill, die, and pay—is an unchanging challenge to state actors: it is the problem for which civil religion, among other things, has been part of the solution.

But consider the context of a globalized world in which political and economic decision makers must secure that sort of primary allegiance. Traditional norms of nationalism, in which the welfare of the individual, family, and community are tied to the health of the state, are subverted by neoliberal state and corporate action that encourages firms to shift production and employment to wherever will optimize net profits—leaving whole communities and regions to wither and disintegrate. In fact, older versions of nationalism—for example, those in which "buy American" was a popular rally cry—*must* be overturned in the interest of global competitiveness and lean-and-mean management systems, even if it means economic suicide for entire regions, industries, and sectors. To be replaced by what? Cheering for "our" firm? "Our" global capitalism? "Our" speculation-fueled stock market? Clearly the need exists for a stronger bond than the thin and dubious enthusiasms generated by the global economy itself.

Similarly, given the negative consequences of domestic neoliberal philosophy—abandonment of the poor, stagnant real wages for the majority, rapidly increased levels of economic and political inequality—the need to reaffirm that there is an "us" in the United States is stronger than ever. In the face of cultural diversity, economic stratification, and the like, some way to make real a sense of community—however much "imagined" in might be, in Benedict Anderson's sense of the term—is an explicit need voiced by pundits and policy makers alike.

Finally, the extent to which external military threats must be exaggerated, stage-managed, and sold to domestic consumers itself testifies to the erosion of stronger forms of patriotic energy available to state actors in previous eras. In a world where Grenada, Panama, and Iraq must be inflated to the level of grave security threats, in which proxy wars and low-intensity conflicts become first choice due to the less-than-stable public support for full-fledged invasion, some renewed sources of public unity and identity must be constructed or exploited. And make no mistake about it—a globalized world requires liberal use of the sword, Kantian notions of perpetual peace notwithstanding. As noted by one of our least favorite commentators, Thomas Friedman of the *New York Times* (1999):

> The hidden hand of the market will never work without a hidden fist—McDonald's cannot flourish without McDonnell Douglas, the builder of the F-15. And the hidden fist that keeps the world safe for Silicon Valley's technologies is called the U.S. Army, Air Force, Navy and Marine Corps.

What globalization has done, among other things, is to increase the need for new or renewed sources of social legitimation and cohesion. U.S. political discourse, scholarly and popular, gorges itself with worries about low voter turnout, declining civic involvement, alienation, and individualism. (See Robert Putnam's popular "bowling alone" metaphor to describe the rise of privatized culture over communal forms like "bowling on a team." We once attended a conference at which Putnam's "bowling alone" metaphor was invoked so often that we decided to skip an afternoon of lectures to go bowling—together.) In light of these and related problems of "civic virtue," religion now appears in a newer, more positive light. While the cruder forms of American civil religion are clearly inadequate, newer forms—under different names—are being constructed, and the public participation of religious communities is courted, albeit under rather restricted terms of offer.

The terms of contemporary discussion, however, hardly ever use the term "civil religion"—for some, it is an unseemly term, low on authentic religion and long on a crass sort of nation-worship. Instead, across the disciplines and in church circles, we are witnessing a flowering of debate on how "religion in general"—a telling term in many ways—and Christianity in particular can contribute to revitalizing "civil society," even "global civil society," to the upbuilding of "social capital," to the enhancement of the public square, to new sorts of communitarianism, to a new "social covenant," and more. Any and all of these sound much more noble, much more positive, and much more theologically substantive than the package of connotations carried by the term "civil religion."

Join the Party—If You Don't Cause Trouble

This invitation for an enhanced public role for religious groups and institutions comes from groups and scholars that span the ideological mainstream. It finds expression in the increased role of so-called faith-based organizations (FBO) in matters of social service provision after 1996, in the presidential campaign platforms of both George W. Bush and Al Gore, and in other contexts. Oldline Catholic liberals like Andrew Greeley extol the utility of religion as a source of much-needed social capital, which he defines as the "stock of social relations and shared values that enable people to cooperate." Religious practice builds social capital in many ways, according to Greeley, and it contributes to high levels of volunteerism, generosity, civic responsibility, and ethical concern. As he writes, "This generous religiously driven 'habit of the heart' makes a major contribution to the economy and to the general welfare of the country" (1997).

Many other names could be mentioned here—Michael Perry, Stephen Carter, Francis Fukuyama, James Coleman, and Richard Neuhaus—in a similar fashion. For most of them, the hope is that religion in general and Christianity in particular—under certain circumstances, anyway—might provide the civic virtue, the bonds of common purpose, the remedies for the political, economic, and cultural fragmentation associated with the brave new globalized world.

No doubt many people, especially in the churches, will be offended by our claim that late-imperial America welcomes Christianity only in a highly subordinated and instrumental posture. While we will examine many manifestations of compromised Christianity in later chapters, we find many of our claims illustrated and vindicated by a rather unlikely source that deserves mention here.

The Heritage Foundation is among the most powerful Washington-based public policy centers and think tanks. Backed by corporate gifts and conservative foundations, Heritage can justly claim significant impact on national policy on a variety of issues. And while its approach on some issues defines the rightward edge of respectable Beltway policy making, we are impressed with how its thinking on religion and society converges with more liberal political voices on objectives, if not tactics.

Especially revealing as a statement of how established powers—in this case, speaking with a conservative accent, but an establishment voice nonetheless—see religion is a 1996 background paper published and distributed widely by Heritage. "Why Religion Matters: The Impact of Religious Practice on Social Stability" was written by Patrick F. Fagan, senior fellow in family and cultural issues at Heritage and a prominent social policy analyst. Amid the recent flurry of books and articles calling for the renewal of civil society and communitarian ethics, Fagan summarizes research on the social consequences of religious beliefs and practices. Religion is a solution to (or protection against) a vast array of social problems, according to Fagan.

Indeed, Fagan claims that religious practice can help America deal with issues that include marital stability, divorce, sexual satisfaction and marital happiness, suicide, drug abuse, out-of-wedlock pregnancy, crime, and alcoholism. It can also help move poor inner-city individuals out of poverty, boost low self-esteem, improve physical health, and lessen the likelihood of contracting several fatal diseases.

Fagan finds that "religious practice contributes significantly to the quality of American life." It is so useful and helpful, providing so many benefits and cost savings to the polity that it may even have national security implications: "the peace and happiness of the nation depend significantly on a renewal of religious practice and belief."

Where Fagan parts company with his more liberal partners in the political mainstream is in his call for greater state promotion of religiosity. Given the overwhelming evidence for the social utility of religion, Fagan makes recommendations that the President, Congress, and Supreme Court should act to increase religious practice as a way to deal with a range of social pathologies and problems. For their part, religious leaders should emphasize the patriotic aspects of their faith in dealing with congregations and would-be members. Church leaders "should make clear to their congregations that they are contributing not only to their own welfare, but also to the well-being of the nation by their regular attendance at religious worship." The alliance of self-interest and social stability is apparent also in the links Fagan sees between frequent religious practice and happiness. "Happy people tend to be productive and law-abiding. They learn well, make good citizens, and are invariably pleasant people."

For persons sensitive to the integrity of the gospel and the mission of the church, Fagan's approach (and the mainstream assumptions it reflects) cannot go unchallenged; in fact, much of this book stands as a critique of such a view of the church. Nowhere in his paper does Fagan define what "religion" is, nor does he distinguish much between various religions and denominations—in a footnote, he notes his use of "church" and "churchgoer" in the "generic sense" to refer to any sort of institutional religiosity. The only conceptual distinction evident in his understanding of religion is between "intrinsic" and "extrinsic" religious behavior. Intrinsic religion is "God-oriented and based on belief which transcends the person's own existence." This sort of religious practice and belief is good, with beneficial consequences for individual, state, and society. Extrinsic religion is "self-oriented and characterized by outward observance, not internalized as a guide to behavior and attitudes." This is bad religion, with consequences worse than no religion at all.

While Fagan's diffuse, generalized notion of what constitutes proper religion seems pluralistic and open, in fact it excludes many important traditions and perspectives. For example, we doubt that Jesus of Nazareth—or those who have internalized his priorities, practices, and affections as their way of life—would pass muster with Fagan as a practitioner of "intrinsic religion" as defined by its social outcomes. After all, in his own time and place, Jesus was seen as a threat to family stability, the peace and tranquillity of the imperial order, and the pursuit of wealth, personal gain, and self-esteem.

Those who, like Jesus, seek first the kingdom of God instead of lesser gods and loyalties do not necessarily enjoy better sex, more income, or patriotic accolades. They do tend to encounter the cross and sometimes martyrdom, which are not among the socially useful byproducts of religion that Fagan seeks to multiply. Martyrdom, for example, can lead to an increase in single-parent families, orphaned children, and decreases in family income.

In fact, Fagan's sense of what constitutes a proper and healthy religion is ominously close to that of Jesus' opponents, at least those who stood for congenial relations with the Roman overlords. Proper (or, in Fagan's terms, "intrinsic") religiosity leads to order, social peace, and the blessings of family, property, and social respect. Any threat to proper religiosity and its byproducts is pathological and must be extirpated for the good of the community—such is the theology of Caiaphas ("It is to your advantage that one man should die for the people, rather than that the whole nation should perish" John 11:50 NJB), and maybe of Fagan also.

While Fagan assumes that religion should contribute to "the quality of American life," it is not at all obvious from the Christian tradition that enhancing the quality of life for the powerful is the goal of the gospel. On the contrary, the gospel's hostility to wealth and the exploitation it presupposes and enables would seem more likely to criticize and demand alternatives to the "quality" of American life constructed by capitalism. By making contributions to the "quality of American life" a benchmark for religious legitimacy, Fagan is dangerously close to a theology of nation-worship, which from a Christian perspective is *always* idolatrous, *always* in opposition to the loyalty due God and his peace-able kingdom. This sort of idolatry sometimes appears more clearly in the pronouncements of state leaders. For instance, U.S. Secretary of State Madeleine Albright recently proclaimed that "If we have to use force, it is because we are America. We are the indispensable nation" (Longworth, 1998). Such unvarnished arrogance runs afoul of the perspective of the biblical God for whom *no* nation—not even the beloved Israel—is indispensable to the divine plan; if even Israel cannot be indispensable, how much more "dispensable" are the imperial *poseurs* of Babylon, Rome, and Washington, D.C.?

Fagan's worship of the family is similarly inflated. Christians affirm the family and other forms of human community and association—but only derivatively; that is, the family is affirmed only to the extent that it facilitates discipleship and fidelity to God's calling. The Gospel accounts assume, however, that much of the time family arrangements are impediments to discipleship and the radical Way of Jesus. Christians should respect and honor "family values" only when and if those values encourage people in mutual faithfulness, vocation, and the upbuilding of the new community of Christ. When the family has other ends—mere survival, self-preservation at the expense of others, social advancement divorced from sacrificial love—the church must resist it as a tribalism that privileges blood relations over the body of Christ.

None of this, of course, is the sort of Christianity or "religion in general" that Fagan wants to encourage. For him and many other elites caught in the rough water of global political, economic, and cultural currents, the purpose of religion is to boost, support, and unify American society and culture (and the capitalist way of life upon which American power rests). Indeed, Fagan even references one of the most famous articulations of this view (without the slightest hint of irony) when he quotes from George Washington's farewell address:

> Of all the dispositions and habits which lead to political prosperity, religion and morality are indispensable supports. In vain would the man claim the tribute of patriotism who should labor to subvert these great pillars of human happiness—these firmest props

of the duties of men and citizens. . . . Where is the security for prosperity, for reputation, for life, if the sense of religious obligation
desert the oaths which are the instruments of investigation in courts
of justice? And let us with caution indulge the supposition that
morality can be maintained without religion. Whatever may be
conceded to the influence of refined education on minds of peculiar structure, reason and experience both forbid us to expect that
national morality can prevail in exclusion of religious principle.

Like the Roman emperors who turned to Christianity as a salve
for crises of internal order and legitimacy, our current rulers want
a religion that cares without critique and praises without prophetic
denunciation. They want chaplaincy—managed care for the soul,
if you will. And for what Fagan and persons like him want, the
Army's Command Religious Master Plan may be a kind of tem-
plate for organizing, financing, and evaluating the chaplaincy
needed for the entire country.

Toward Christianity Incorporated

As stated earlier, we will concentrate in this book on how the
workings of the world economy in particular steer the Christian
gospel and its expressions into safe, domesticated forms. As states
defer to the prerogatives of corporations in the neoliberal era now
upon us, we are persuaded that the sorts of chaplaincy services
demanded from Christianity will be connected in important ways
to the problems and power disparities produced by capitalism. It
is in this sense that we see the transformation of the church into
a caricature of its best self, something we call "Christianity Incorporated"—a church that has bent to capitalism and economic
power so long that its own practices and beliefs become shaped
by the corporate form and spirit.

We had been working on *Christianity Incorporated* for more than
six months before we found the identical phrase used to describe
the commercial ideal of religion—one that is practical, uplifting,
patriotic, and good for business. We found it in *Babbitt*, Sinclair
Lewis's satirical attack on small-town boosterism, consumerism,

self-promotion, and groupthink. He wrote in and about a time like our own in many respects—businessmen celebrated as heroes, rising stock markets, and governments working to induce loyalty and conformity. Lewis published *Babbitt* in 1922; we hope he won't mind if we keep the phrase for our title.

The remaining chapters in this book will give examples of Christianity Incorporated in action, of the peculiar cross-dressing in which the church further internalizes the ideologies and practices of for-profit firms while those same firms increasingly utilize religious and Christian symbols, stories, and meaning structures in pursuit of corporate advantage. In this we overlap only partially with existing scholarly literature on ecclesiology and organizational theory, for example the literature on "institutional isomorphism" (see DiMaggio and Powell, 1991). We are aware that "religious" and "nonreligious" movements and structures have borrowed from and imitated one another variously throughout history, but in our view insufficient attention has been directed toward the theological assumptions and consequences attendant to contemporary manifestations of such isomorphic practices.

Unlike much of that literature, we are not focused on the so-called secularization debate (e.g., Cormode, 1998). For us, the question is more modest and more ecclesiocentric: What aspects of contemporary capitalism encourage for-profit corporations to exploit Christian and religious cultural resources? What sorts of ecclesiology impel the churches to imitate the tools and values of for-profit firms? What does all of this portend for the mission and message of the church conceived of as a movement serving the promised kingdom of God?

Chapter 2, "Putting Jesus to Work: When Corporations Get Religion," explores how the corporate "spirituality and work" movement aims to help workers adjust—quietly and without rebellion—to the downsized, reengineered, and transnationalized nature of contemporary capitalism. Chapter 3, "The Political Economy of Formation," examines the conflict between churches and for-profit "culture industries" over the shaping of human attitudes, dispositions, and practices. Our fourth chapter, "The Church and the Death Business," focuses on an area of church life and practice—Christian funerals, burials, and care for the dead—

recently under attack from corporate conglomerates, but where the outcome is not yet certain.

Chapters 5 and 6 focus more directly on the intellectual and theological assumptions—faulty, in our view—facilitating the subordination of the church to capitalist democracy. "John Locke in Ecclesial Drag? The Problems with *Centesimus Annus*," offers our critique of this major Catholic statement on matters of Christianity and capitalism. We extend this discussion into major Protestant bodies in chapter 6, entitled "Church as Citizen, Church as Chaplain."

As Christian writers, we do not believe that God abandons the world or the church, no matter how far either strays from God. The final chapter of this book, "Toward an Economics of Discipleship: The Church as *Oikos*," begins to identify some elements appropriate for an ecclesial economic ethic not beholden to the coercion and domination in Christianity Incorporated. We derive these provisional elements from a source not usually seen as a font of Christian insight on economic practices—namely, the Sermon on the Mount. Our purpose is not to offer a full scale economic model (indeed, such is almost certainly a bad idea at this stage), nor to twist the Sermon in a disrespectful sort of prooftexting. Rather it is more modest: to open space for further development, to encourage our brothers and sisters in Christ to see beyond the self-fulfilling "inevitability" of Christianity Incorporated, and to work for an economics of discipleship more in service to the promised kingdom of God.

It may be relevant to note something about our own ecclesial associations. We are both Roman Catholic laymen whose work aims to serve the entire church across reformational and denominational lines. One of us is a political economist, the other is a philosopher, and we are two of the leaders of The Ekklesia Project, an ecumenical gathering of Christian scholars, pastors, and laypeople committed to more robust notions of discipleship and the church. The Ekklesia Project is one effort among others working to chart a future for Christianity that is different from that being forged by the relentless move toward Christianity Incorporated. We invite you to "taste and see" for yourself at <www.ekklesiaproject.org>.

2

Putting Jesus to Work:
When Corporations Get Religion

ook inside the engine of corporate capitalism—into the workplaces, offices, cubicles, and warehouses—and you will see some of the paradoxes of the neoliberal era.

On the outside, things couldn't be better. The stock market, after its gravity-defying climb of the 1990s, has shifted to an up-and-down ride even as official unemployment and inflation levels in the United States remain uncommonly low. The presidential campaign of 2000 in the United States played out with the incumbent party claiming "peace and prosperity" as its legacy of the 1990s.

But beneath the surface, things are unsettled. Workers who should be happy are insecure, anxious about the future, and harboring high levels of animosity toward their firms. Having survived the liquidation of their coworkers and friends as wave after wave of "downsizing," "reengineering," and "flexibility" washed over them, millions of working people in the United States and elsewhere are far from jubilant. Stockholders and corporate raiders may be dancing, but many of those under them seem overworked, alienated, and cynical (see Cooper, 1999, pp. 115–8).

Executives who saw stock prices rise in tandem with layoffs must now confront an array of unwanted byproducts of such strategies. Their firms are lean, but often their employees are mean. Having disabused both blue- and white-collar employees

27

of the outdated notion of employment security in exchange for loyal and productive service, capitalist firms have reshuffled the cards of personnel management, employee creativity, and labor control.

This picture will seem odd or obsolete to persons convinced by the news media and political leaders that economic expansion has showered benefits upon all workers. In fact, while pundits some-time talk as if stock markets rise indefinitely and recessions are a thing of the past, the working men and women who experienced the scorching downsizing of the past decade may not be so for-getful (*Worklife Report*, 1999, pp. 4–5). Most people in the work world do not labor in a dynamic dotcom world (which went from boom to bust on its own), most do not enjoy stock options worth millions of dollars, and most do not work in secure, pampered workplaces. The corporate community itself testifies to the con-tradictory trends shaping life in intensified market societies. While some bravely point to evidence of rising employee morale and increased levels of job satisfaction—typical in any economic upturn, to some degree (see for example Leonard, 2000, pp. 29–30; *Management Services*, 2000, pp. 5–6)—other corporate strategists fret over how to wring value out of burned-out, over-worked, and demoralized employees.

There are plenty of work opportunities these days—so many, in fact, that increased numbers of families in the United States work more than one job per adult member. For millions of fam-ilies, multiple wage-earners and multiple jobs have been the forces that have only now pushed real incomes for the majority back to their early-1970s levels. Even as official statistics continue to underestimate poverty and unemployment, job growth contin-ues to be strong in part-time, casual, and temporary work—typ-ically involving low wages, no security, and usually no benefits. It is in such a paradoxical and contradictory era that labor "short-ages" are front-page news (such shortages, especially in service sectors like fast food and janitorial work, tend to vanish when wages move up from their present below-poverty levels), where "consumer confidence" is reported as strong, and where employ-ees are smiling on the outside but oftentimes scowling on the inside. How to get such people to work hard, to invest themselves in their efforts, continues to be a problem in spite of economic cheerleading to the contrary.

Earlier in the twentieth century, business leaders developed contrasting—but not incompatible—ways to deal with such problems. The iron-fist approach to labor management was exemplified by the "scientific management" approach associated with Frederick Taylor. Workers were subjected to intense scrutiny, work processes were deskilled and routinized by machines and process engineers, and an army of foremen enforced the "time-and-motion" dictates of the production experts.

The velvet glove of business control focused more on inducements than overt coercion. The "human relations" approaches of Elton Mayo and others developed an arsenal of programs, seminars, counseling services, and resources, all reflecting the assumption that keeping workers happy, healthy, and cared-for makes them productive, loyal, and docile. Whatever the ups and downs of the world economy and countless management fads, capitalist firms have employed combinations of Taylor and Mayo alternately to whip and entice production workers, clerical staff, and sales forces. With the coming of more intense global markets in the past twenty-five years, advanced telecommunications and computers have turned the tools of labor management back upon hundreds of thousands of corporate managers, supervisors, and data-crunchers who once thought themselves relatively safe from the fates they visited on their subordinates.

What was once a peculiarly American system of labor utilization—easy hiring and firing, with management demands for "flexible" labor markets supported by the state—looks to become the norm even in places that scorned such an approach as an unnecessarily barbaric style of capitalist practice. Neoliberal political pressure via the International Monetary Fund, World Trade Organization, and other U.S.-dominated institutions combine with internal problems to force the abandonment of "lifetime" employment in Japan, a system very different than that of the United States, even though it never embraced a majority of Japanese workers at its peak. Similarly, Western European political and corporate leaders can't run fast enough from whatever social democratic compromises they once supported, deals that granted a measure of employment security and labor empowerment in the workplace. The American model of instant hires and fires, a small core of valued workers surrounded by a reserve army of rapidly deployed temporary, part-time, and casual workers, is coming to typify corporations across industrial sectors and national boundaries.

While most large firms now have fewer employees relative to output, they do not have fewer problems with personnel management, control, and motivation. Depending on the industry, the problems may be becoming more, not less, pressing. Human resources writer Jennifer Laabs sums up the situation:

> As companies have downsized, restructured and reorganized themselves into oblivion, they've been left with skeleton crews who, quite literally, feel lifeless, tired and sucked dry. Managers struggle to manage work forces with little energy, creativity, or commitment. . . .
>
> Despite the fact that fewer people are doing more work, managers still demand everything they used to demand, and more . . . In a world where companies no longer commit to workers for life, and vice-versa, what's left to consummate the bonding process? (1995, p. 62)

"Consummating the bonding process," as Laabs puts it, is a major corporate preoccupation these days, being pursued even while global capitalism continues to erode the positions of most workers in advanced industrial countries. While businesses explore many ways to blur the contradictions and mollify their surviving personnel, we find especially interesting the proliferation of "spirituality and work" initiatives that seek to provide meaning, peace of mind, inspiration, and pastoral care to their workers—all from the company store, of course.

Whatever the economic benefits of capitalist firms trading in transcendence, we are convinced such activities represent more bad news for persons concerned with the integrity and viability of the gospel in our time. While capitalism as a system has always attempted to enlist the support of religion in its cause—with varying degrees of success—these contemporary attempts to exploit spirituality and religion take on increased significance when viewed in a larger context of changing relations between capitalism and cultural institutions and traditions (see Budde, 1997). Cultural symbols, narratives, images, and experiences are being exploited in ever more diverse and creative ways by firms attempting to intensify both production and consumption in ways conducive to corporate profitability. The corporate trade in transcendence raises profound theological, pastoral, and social questions for churches and other religious institutions. Unless they recognize these moves for what they are, the slide of religious institutions and communities into triviality and irrelevance will continue unabated. We will examine several expressions of the corporate appropriation of spirituality, Christianity, and matters of the soul.

Finding God at Work

Theorists and publicists of corporate spirituality initiatives promote their movement in terms of employee empowerment, self-esteem, and the desire to transcend limits. According to Judith A. Neal, editor of the quarterly newsletter *Spirit at Work* and a professor at the University of New Haven:

> Spirituality at work is about people seeing their work as a spiritual path, as an opportunity to grow personally and to contribute to society in a meaningful way. It is about learning to be more caring and compassionate with fellow employees, with bosses, with subordinates and customers. It is about integrity, being true to oneself, and telling the truth to others. Spirituality in the workplace can refer to an individual's attempts to live his or her values more fully in the workplace. Or it can refer to the ways in which organizations structure themselves to support the spiritual growth of employees (1997, p. 123).

An untold number of books, seminars, in-house workshops, and experiences now exist to meet what Pamela Leigh calls "the longing to create a workplace where everyone from the top down shares a unified vision and sense of purpose beyond making money" (1997, p. 26). While no exact figures are available, experts within the human relations field report dramatic increases in the number of such programs offered and produced (see Brandt, 1996; Leigh, 1997, p. 26; Fleckler Feltz, 1993, p. 5).

What's done in corporate spirituality programs ranges from the traditional to the esoteric to the trendy. One consultancy uses "images, concepts and perception-altering exercises" from Navajo, Sioux, Apache, and other Native American traditions; its clients include IBM, Honeywell, and Bethlehem Steel (Brandt, 1996). Other practices include nature walks, inspirational seminars, meditation, yoga, uplifting literature, journal-writing, and "positive visualization" exercises (see Neal, 1997, p. 137; Neck and Milliman, 1994).

One important distinction noted by nearly all corporate spirituality advocates is between spirituality (which is good) and religion (which is usually bad). Whereas religion is particularistic, dogmatic, exclusionary, and rife with First Amendment problems, spirituality is universal, accommodating, inclusive, and personally empowering. Some of the remaining corporate hesitation regarding business spirituality programs is the product of misunderstanding, according to Neal: some human resource managers continue to confuse the "S-word, spirituality . . . with the R-word, religion" (Brandt, 1996).

Her view is shared by other spokespersons. Laabs, who calls corporate spirituality "the newest paradigm," stresses that it "isn't about believing in a particular religion . . . It's about taking a broader, more global view of the spiritual dimension which may, for some, encompass their religious beliefs." She cites one survey in *Personnel Journal* in which 40 percent of human resource managers report having policies in place that prohibit bringing or wearing religious symbols or artifacts in the workplace (1995, pp. 65, 68), presumably to avoid First Amendment conflicts and litigation.

The spirituality vs. religion dichotomy is promoted by one of the most popular purveyors of capitalist spirituality. Deepak Chopra, a bestselling author and favorite speaker of many sales executives, argues that organized religion cannot provide spiritual comfort. "Organized religion is about judgment, rules, guilt, fear. Spirituality is about freedom from the above." Chopra promises attendees at his three-day seminar that he will teach them how to attain "the miraculous and the spontaneous fulfillment of your desires." Unlike the punishing self-denial of traditional religion, one of Chopra's lackeys urges conference attendees to "give attention to yourself, the greatest act of self-love" (Jordan, 1997).

The conflict between the sort of spirituality fostered by firms and the reactionary forces of traditional religion will escalate as the former grows, according to Craig Neal. He is founder and president of the Heartland Institute, which is described as "an educational organization that fosters social and spiritual transformation."

"We're going to run into conflict with organized religion," says Neal. "After all, in any true paradigm shift, you're going to have friction, which is necessary for growth" (Leigh, 1997, p. 32).

Indeed, according to some management analysts, the firm has come to imitate, if not replace, the role of the church:

> The [leadership] team becomes the secular equivalent of the religious sect, as a means of resocializing individuals within the workplace. . . . Rational, individual economic interests are insufficient to deliver the levels of commitment required to meet the competition. All strong sects require a "confession of faith" as the basis for their cohesion and commitment; hence the proliferation of mission statements communicating the values of the organization to its members, and the little catechism carried in the staff handbook (Ackers and Preston, 1997, p. 685).

Not everyone in the corporate spirituality movement is opposed to established religious institutions as long as they can be made supportive of company goals and worldviews. It remains true, however, that privileging spirituality over religion—with the former conceived of as a privatized, individualistic, self-improvement project—enables firms to attempt employee personality and character management in ways that may be more difficult if traditional religious communities are the vehicle in question.

The bottom line of corporate interest in spirituality, religiosity, or values is, of course, the bottom line. An expansive case for corporate spirituality programs comes from Christopher Neck and John Milliman (1994):

> Spirituality can positively affect employee and organizational performance in several ways. First, spirituality can lead individuals to experience consciousness at a deeper level, thereby enhancing their intuitive abilities. Intuition, in turn, is considered an important leadership and management skill which is related to personal and organizational productivity. . . .
>
> Second, spirituality-based intuition can also facilitate employees [sic] to develop a more purposeful and compelling organizational vision, which can also increase innovation. . . . In addition, organizations with a spiritual mission are often able to attract and retain the most creative employees. Third, organizations which offer spirituality-oriented work goals provide opportunities for employees to experience a higher sense of service and greater personal growth and development. In turn, the sense of growth can significantly increase employee energy and enthusiasm. . . .
>
> Fourth, spiritual-based values can enhance teamwork and employee commitment to the organization, attributes which are highly sought after by corporate executives in the USA—a country which has a highly individualistic culture. By meeting personal needs, a compelling spiritual vision can also create a strong bond between the employees and the company, thereby enhancing employee motivation and teamwork and commitment to the organization's goals.

Leigh notes that "emphasizing values has proved profitable in measurable ways" for many firms—affecting conventional concerns like absenteeism, turnover, and recruitment, but also in inspiring workers to be more creative and responsible on the job in ways that boost quality and competitiveness (1997, pp. 31–32). Beneath the lofty aims of the corporate spirituality movement lives capitalism's enduring need to maximize labor's output at the lowest possible cost. If matters of the soul are relevant to that, then matters of the soul must be added to the corporate repertoire—along with old reliables like firings, goon squads, workplace surveillance, and incentive/disincentive structures. The firm's interest in employee spirituality is derivative from its more fundamental view of employees as resources to be exploited in the most efficient ways possible. As noted by Breuer (1997):

> After all, employees are investments. Just as a company would try to get to the heart of a machinery failure problem, it should also view employee failure in the same light. It often just takes a lot more finesse to diagnose and solve the problem.

One particularly ambitious program that blends the "power of positive thinking" with 90s-style psychological and management jargon comes from Neck and Milliman. In the *Journal of Managerial Psychology* (1994), the pair describe their technique of Thought Self-Leadership (TSL), which they describe as a way to "empower employees with the skills to control and enhance their perceptions about work, and thus gain more spirituality in their organizational life." TSL takes "positive thinking"—change your outlook, not power relations or social conditions—to new heights (or depths), as its goal is to help workers "identify and confront their dysfunctional beliefs and replace them with more rational beliefs." In particular, TSL techniques include

> self-management of individual self-dialogue (what we covertly tell ourselves), mental imagery (the creation and, in essence, symbolic experience of imagined results of our behaviour before we actually perform), and beliefs and assumptions (distorted individual beliefs may be the basis of dysfunctional thought processes).

Neck and Milliman mention (but do not elaborate upon) empirical evidence that supports their claim that

> employees who participate in a TSL training intervention . . . experienced enhanced mental performance, affective states, job satisfaction and self-efficiency expectations over those not receiving the training.

Whatever the quality of such "empirical evidence"—one wonders how the authors operationalize "enhanced mental performance" or enhanced "affective states"—the popularity of their sort of endeavor testifies to the lengths to which some major firms will go to address the problems of employment and work in contemporary capitalism. Remolding the psychological and spiritual disposition of employees is a tempting, potentially cost-effective corporate strategy, even while the prospects for success seem far smaller than claimed by Neck, Milliman, and other enthusiasts.

There now exist many ambitious—some critics say totalitarian (Willmott, 1993)—programs aimed at remolding managers' personalities and spiritual foundations in the interest of the firm. Some of these borrow from extreme forms of Japanese retreat experiences (strenuous physical, emotional, and psychological stresses that often leave participants crying hysterically in front of their superiors), others push employees toward quasireligious conversion experiences at the request of the company (Ackers and Preston, 1997, pp. 689–89). These and more restrained types of Management Development (MD) programs have, according to two scholars familiar with them, "entered an emotional and existential terrain that appeals to similar ideas of self-discovery, faith and commitment" (Ackers and Preston, 1977, p. 689) typical of religious conversions.

While participation in authentic religious conversion processes is voluntary, Peter Ackers and Diane Preston note that

> there is obvious pressure on employees to go along with the whims of their employer and attend the most recent HRM [Human Resource Management] initiative or, if they belong to the group labeled managers, to participate in the most radical MD programmes. . . . Managers are selected and promoted on the basis of desired organizational behaviour and beliefs. In reality, their submission to, and participation in, MD programmes may signal vulnerability, not power (1997, p. 689).

In deemphasizing the cold rationalism of a Weberian approach to corporate management by increasing attention to emotional and affective factors of corporate culture, firms seek to direct and deepen employees' loyalty to the firm—a goal not as different from the Weberian bureaucratic model as Ackers and Preston seem to suggest. "The new management language of cathartic personal change, of re-discovering self, of breaking old personal barriers, of commencing a personal journey, of having utopian visions, reprises a much more ancient tradition of religious imagery," especially of Christian conversion and vocation (Ackers and Preston, 1997, pp. 684, 687). These sorts of MD programs attempt to foster (with varying degrees of success and long-term impact) a secular conversion experience once thought to be beyond the appropriate limits of Western corporate behavior: "It is one thing to be asked to address your own shortcomings in terms of the gap between actual and desired management behaviour; it is quite another matter to be boxed into considering ways in which your personality might be remoulded to fit that desired by your employer" (1997, p. 689).

Ackers and Preston note that

> MD programmes which expose employees to very obvious physical or psychological damage are easy targets for criticism. Equally, this disquiet is quickly dismissed as an hysterical reaction to the work of a few cranks, as with popular fears about religious cults. Yet, the concern remains that a diluted, more subtle and plausible version of the same game has crept into the spirit of more mainstream MD activity. . . . Some major business organizations are engaged in these maverick activities (1997, p. 690).

Most corporate spirituality programs do not go as far as Neck and Milliman's goal of "changing one's core beliefs," or those studied by Ackers and Preston that attempt to "claim the souls" of managers. Another blossoming, albeit more modest, expression of the spirituality and work movement is the field of corporate chaplaincy services and programs. In many ways these are an extension of the existing employee assistance program (EAP) model, in which a firm provides a variety of social services to employees in order to keep them healthy, productive, and reliable. EAP-style programs have recognized that the workplace is the primary institution in most people's lives (eclipsing religious

and community institutions, as well as the family), and offer help
with problems ranging from alcoholism and substance abuse to
family difficulties, stress management, and cigarette smoking.

The replacement of existing religious and civic groups by corporations is acknowledged by many in the corporate spirituality
movement. There are business advantages to this shift in roles,
laments about the decline of "civil society" notwithstanding. As
noted by Laabs:

> In the past, an individual might have turned to his or her religious
> community, civic group or family. But nowadays, the workplace
> is many people's main source for connection and contribution.
> That shift provides employers with a genuine opportunity to
> cement employees' loyalty and service (1997, p. 28).

Other human resource analysts see a similar trend. Nancy
Breuer, a Los Angeles-based consultant with graduate degrees in
theology and management, sees religious groups and pastors being
displaced by workplace human resource agencies. Work demands
more time from employees (a point supported by the economist
Juliet Schor, 1991, among others), hence making the workplace
and home the primary places of involvement. "As the workplace
absorbs more roles in employees' lives, including becoming the
primary source of affiliations and friendships, it carries the pressures of those roles" (Breuer, 1997). The company thus becomes
one's pastor, confessor, and counselor, but manages those roles
with workplace productivity as the ultimate point of reference,
not necessarily the best interests of the individual.

For these and related reasons, chaplaincy programs are becoming increasingly common in secular American firms, both as in-
house and subcontracted endeavors. Growing numbers of firms
now see chaplains as a "bottom-line benefit," as another way to
"improve productivity among employees" (Flecker-Feltz, 1993,
p. 5). While a firm like R. J. Reynolds Tobacco (now RJR Nabisco)
has offered full-time chaplains since 1949, the field has seen substantial growth over the past decade. Marketplace Ministries, a
Dallas consultancy that supplies chaplains to firms, reports its
client list has nearly doubled since 1990, and it now contracts

with 132 firms in 38 states. Overall, according to the National Institute of Business and Industrial Chaplains, more than 4,000 clergy work in workplaces (see *USA Today,* 1997, p. 1-B); overall totals are likely higher when volunteer and irregular chaplains are included.

Mark Cress, a onetime maker of pro-business documentaries for syndicated television, is typical of many providers of corporate chaplaincy services. Within eighteen months of founding Inner Activities Ministry (IAM) in 1996, he has established himself as a major provider of chaplain services to firms in the Research Park Triangle area of Raleigh-Durham, North Carolina. He charges employers from $16 to $180 per employee, depending on firm size and the services under contract (Welles, 1997).

Despite the difficulty of the job—helping overworked, overstressed employees in ways that accord with profitability, productivity, and employee retention—Cress is bullish on the industry. "This could potentially be a $100-million-a-year operation," he said. "I'm convinced we'll minister to 1 million people over the next 10 years. You'll be able to track it. The need's too great; the demand is not going to go away." Cress is quick to point out that, despite such talk, IAM is a nonprofit organization rather than a for-profit firm. Where the latter has a business plan, Cress notes, IAM has "a strategic ministry plan." He chose the Raleigh-Durham area to begin his chaplaincy business after discovering it had a higher-than-average number of new business starts (Welles, 1997).

And while clergy and chaplains may be beneficial to individual workers in times of personal crisis, the fundamental corporate objective frames the employee-chaplain relationship. As noted by George Schuman, president of the American Association of Ministry in the Workplace,

> From the corporate perspective, it's a matter of how many man hours can a chaplain save a company by meeting with the employee on the job site (Fleckler-Feltz, 1993, p. 5).

It remains an unspoken truth that, whatever their personal sympathies, corporate chaplains keep to individual issues and prob-

lems. There is little room for clergy who might call into question
the fundamental assumptions of the institution and its arrangements, the rights of management or ownership, or the legitimacy
of corporate capitalism itself—no matter how relevant such large-
level questions might be to the problems brought to the chaplains
by individuals distressed by their roles in the enterprise. Like all
forms of chaplaincy, the focus remains on the micro-level of discrete problems; the legitimacy of institutions and power relations
is out of bounds.

Still another aspect of chaplaincy involves providing uplift, consolation, and affirmation to persons in power. The spiritual comfort needed by those at the top is not the same as that intended
for middle-managers and employees even lower in the hierarchy.
Those who, while taking home huge sums of money in executive
compensation, must fire tens of thousands of wage-earners or
abandon entire communities to destitution often need to be
affirmed as ethical, spiritually sensitive persons forced to make
hard decisions for the good of the shareholders (or "stakehold-
ers," if the executive's sense of responsibility extends a bit further).

One notable program that addresses the spiritual needs and
uneasy consciences of corporate leaders is the Woodstock Business Conference (WBC), associated with the Woodstock Theological Center at the Jesuit-run Georgetown University. The WBC
office in Washington provides a standardized meeting format,
study and discussion materials to its thirteen local chapters. Program topics include questions of compensation, corporate loyalty,
downsizing, and the role of faith in contemporary society. Its objective, according to its executive director James L. Nolan, a onetime
corporate attorney, is

> to help business leaders focus on their work as a call from God and
> move toward greater authenticity. [The WBC] mission is to estab-
> lish and lead a national organization of business executives to
> explore the Judeo-Christian tradition in order:
>   • to assist the individual to integrate faith, family and profes-
> sional life;

- to help the leadership of the firm to develop a corporate culture consistent with Judeo-Christian values; and
- to aid business leaders and corporations to exercise a beneficial influence upon society at large (Nolan, 1996).

Funding for the WBC has drawn from corporate and foundation grants and membership dues (which begin at $300 per year). At an intellectual level, the WBC continually affirms the compatibility of corporate profitability with ethical decision making and Judeo-Christian values (especially Catholic social teaching on capital and labor). While stressing the difficulties confronting executives who seek to reconcile these objectives in concrete circumstances, the WBC affirms that doing good and doing well are both possible and necessarily linked. Like other Catholic corporate concerns, the WBC has drawn legitimation for its recent work from *Centesimus Annus,* Pope John Paul II's 1991 revision of papal teaching on capitalism (we explore the significance and deficiencies of *Centesimus Annus* in chapter 5).

For all its intellectual ambition and emphasis, one suspects that much of the appeal of the WBC and similar groups lies in the old-fashioned comfort, reassurance, and affirmation it provides to the successful corporate leaders who are its members. The group's primary brochure, for example, mentions the business person's need for "peace of mind" three different times. It also takes note—twice—of the "sleepless nights" they experience. Both themes—peace of mind and being able to sleep without a troubled conscience—appear intermittently in the group's regular newsletter. By joining the WBC, corporate leaders can learn to combine a sense of business as a divinely blessed vocation with the primary vocation to make a profit (see brochure at <adminweb.georgetown.edu/woodstock/wbc/wbc-in.htm>).

While TSL-style manipulations and employee chaplaincy programs might define the high and low intensity ranges of corporate spirituality efforts (with WBC-style programs combining affirmation with topical discussions closer to the low end), the middle range seems to be occupied by a plethora of short-term seminars, symposia, workshops, retreats, and booster sessions. While such experiences used to be targeted mostly at the legions of corporate sales representatives—whose self-esteem, enthusiasm, and ability to rise above rejection made their emotional states a matter of bottom-line corporate concern—large numbers of corporations drag or entice many if not all levels of staff through such programs.

The Peter Lowe International Company, for instance, runs a series of "Success Seminars," which expose several hundred thousand executives a year to an all-star roster of athletes, politicians, and military leaders with inspiring stories to tell and wisdom to impart. To Lowe, spirituality

> is all about thinking positively and having a good impression of yourself. . . . Salespeople find spirituality because it is a method to defeat failures. You can't win in business until you have a positive concept of yourself.

When an interviewer suggests to Lowe that many business winners don't think of themselves as being spiritual or religious, Lowe responds: "But I bet they think pretty highly of themselves" (Cohen, 1997).

Lowe, whose seminars are a full nine hours of motivational talks (and promotions for the books, tapes, calendars, and other merchandise peddled by his celebrity speakers), concedes that corporate spirituality gurus have an image problem ("hucksters") to overcome. Nonetheless, he remains upbeat about the real needs programs like his address:

> Spirituality gives people something to grasp onto, and in an age when downsizing has taken over and job security is at an all-time low, that's what they are looking for. There's a desperation in life today that spirituality is helping to heal (Cohen, 1997).

Lowe's competitors in the spirituality and work industry make similar claims. Deepak Chopra offers a social vision in tune with the increased inequality that accompanies the current era of capitalist vigor. "Spirituality and wealth-consciousness go hand in hand," he tells one conference crowd. "Poverty is a reflection of an impoverished spirit" (Jordan, 1997). Evidently, even classical equations of wealth and virtue (and poverty and character inadequacy) can be translated into the New Age/therapeutic language of our day.

The last example of the corporate capture of Christianity and religiosity is more decentralized and individualistic than the other expressions we have examined. It is found in the proliferation of books offered by publishing conglomerates that seek to derive "management lessons," "leadership insights," or "business wisdom" from Christian experience—most especially from the "life and teaching" of Jesus of Nazareth. While the evangelical subculture has produced a steady stream of "Jesus Wants You to Be Rich" and "How to Run A Christian Company and Make Money" books for years, we are more interested in the expansion of such Jesus-centered business and managerial self-help books beyond the evangelical market. Perhaps the quintessential example here is Laurie Beth Jones, who has leveraged her 1995 bestseller *Jesus CEO: Using Ancient Wisdom for Visionary Leadership* (published by Hyperion Press, a division of the Disney Corporation) into a wide-ranging management consulting, leadership training, and public seminar business targeting businesses, hospitals, government agencies, and nonprofit organizations. She now runs the Jesus CEO Foundation, publishes the *Jesus CEO News* (its motto is "Power You Can Use"), and has trained dozens of facilitators who now spread the Jesus CEO gospel via paid seminars, symposia, and conferences. The approach to business outlined in *Jesus CEO* has expanded via successor volumes to encompass a consulting/training function dedicated to constructing organizational mission statements and effective corporate management systems.

Jones has constructed an impressive edifice with her fellow "spiritreneurs"—a term of self-reference she created that means "highly talented and motivated" persons "who want to use our business talents and skills for the glory of God, yet remain independent from a bureaucracy." Despite the frequent mention of God in her newsletters (aimed at the true believers in her message), Jones's main book on Jesus and management is far from religious in tone or approach (its preface recommends the book to "any business, service, or endeavor that depends on more than one person to accomplish a goal"). The volume is a collection of short (mostly two to four page) chapters with discussion questions at the end of each. Chapter titles describing Jesus' management style include "He Believed in Himself," "He Expressed Himself," "He Formed a Team," "He Took One Step at a Time," "He Was a Turnaround Specialist," "He Was Open to People and Their Ideas," and "He Clearly Defined Their Work-Related Benefits." The text is a painful combination of shallow sentiment, self-help clichés ("If only we believed in ourselves, the world would be a better place," p. 17), and trivialization of the Gospel accounts (she never answers the question of why Jesus drove moneychangers from the temple—among the most politically and theologically charged scenes in the entire New Testament—and instead changes it into a reflection on being a "passionate" leader, pp. 50–54).

Like many other writers in the "Jesus the Business Hero" genre, Jones draws a highly stylized, individualistic, and decidedly Westernized portrait of Jesus. Ironically, a more forthright exposition of Jones's ideas on Christianity and capitalism are offered in an interview in *Industry Week*. She describes what initially attracted her to the topic:

> I was struck by the fact that [Jesus] had only three years to train 12 people—none of whom were divine—to go out and change the world; and that he trained them so effectively that they went on to do the work after he left. I asked, "What did he do with these people to turn them into such lean, clean, marketing machines. What skills did he possess that we could duplicate or learn from?" (Brown, 1995).

Like most spirituality and work enthusiasts, Jones wants religion out of the workplace because it is too particularistic. Further, religion is "necessarily man-made and therefore highly fallible." Similarly, she champions "spirituality" over religion—including Christianity—at work.

> While not everyone is religious, everyone is spiritual, because we are composed of mind, body, and spirit. Therefore our spirit is already in the workplace, because our minds and bodies are. Spir-

itual principles are universal; they can and should be applied everywhere (Brown, 1995).

Out of the entire life and practice of Jesus, Jones distills three principles relevant to corporate management today: self-mastery, action, and relationship skills. Together these comprise the "Omega management style" used by Jesus, which "can be implemented by anyone who dares." These traits, she asserts, could readily fit many secular leaders like Jefferson, Edison, and Theodore Roosevelt. Furthermore,

> Anyone who practices these spiritual principles is bound to experience success. In fact, the study and application of spiritual principles comes with success guaranteed (Brown, 1995).

Jones says corporations should view their employees' spirituality as an "untapped resource," insofar as at least 30 percent of each employee's potential is underutilized. Her advice is for executives to engage spiritual techniques, "and productivity and morale will soar" (Brown, 1995).

What is remarkable about the *Jesus CEO* phenomenon and similar books is their broad acceptance and popularity in publishing and business circles. The prototype for the genre remains the often-cited but little-read *The Man Nobody Knows*, written in 1925 by Bruce Barton. Barton, the cofounder and chair of one of the world's premier advertising agencies (Batten, Barton, Durstine, and Osborne—BBD&O, as it is known in the field), derived leadership and advertising insights from Jesus that could benefit modern executives and promoters.

Like Jones, Barton airlifts Jesus out of his historical context of imperialism, brutal oppression of the poor, and widespread social discontent. Indeed, to Barton, Galilean life "was a cheery and easygoing affair; with them the sun shone almost every day; the land was fruitful; making a living was nothing much to worry about" (pp. 5–6). Barton imagines Jesus to possess a "vigorous physique," with "muscles hard as iron"; in fact, Jesus drove the moneychangers from the temple without interference because observers could tell that "He was fully capable of taking care of Himself" (pp. 6, 21).

Where Jones sees "Omega" management principles in Jesus and great American leaders, Barton illustrates a common tendency in American civil religion by frequently comparing Jesus and Abraham Lincoln in terms of leadership and rhetorical skills. Like Jones, Barton focused on Jesus as a builder and animator of an organization that changed the world—with lessons therein for corporate recruitment, training, and motivation (pp. 2–3, 13, 15). As a pioneer in advertising, Barton was impressed by Jesus' skills at publicity and promotion. Jesus' message

> conquered not because there was any *demand* for another religion but because Jesus knew how, and taught His followers how, to catch the attention of the indifferent, and translate a great spiritual conception into terms of practical self-concern (p. 57).

Indeed, Barton writes, "With anything which is not a basic necessity the supply always precedes the demand." In other words, Jesus knew the "law" of supply and demand to be "misleading" because demand must be created by skillful promotion that convinces people of their need for the new opportunity (p. 49). Except that his work concerned things more important than theirs, Barton asserts, Jesus is most like the modern psychologist and businessman in using "the most modern techniques of overcoming unreasoning resistance to a helpful idea, service or product" (pp. 57–8).

Barton, like Jones, proclaims the compatibility of corporate success with the management precepts of Jesus. According to Barton, making a profit includes being concerned with a customer's pleasure, safety, comfort, and convenience, and convincing the customer of that concern. This concern is the "spirit of modern business," the same thing that Jesus preached nearly two thousand years earlier (p. 90).

Barton's book never enjoyed the commercial success of *Jesus CEO*, although the ad agency he founded dwarfs the cottage industry spawned by Jones. While they share a great deal in terms of approach, Jones dares to tread on topics Barton never touched.

Not even the crucifixion of Jesus—a political execution conducted by the bloody Roman Empire—is beyond utilization as a source of business boosterism and can-do thinking. To wit: "Jesus was such an action-oriented leader that they literally had to nail him down to keep him from doing more" (Brown, 1995).

A Church-Based Critique of Corporate Spirituality

We see much at stake for the Christian community in the array of corporate incursions into spirituality, religiosity, and matters of "ultimate meaning." Our concerns are different from those within the business world who criticize such moves on the grounds of irrelevance, inappropriateness, or incompetence (see Micklethwait and Wooldridge, 1996; Austin, 1995). Rather, we are concerned with how the corporate exploitation of faith and meaning will contribute to the further trivialization of Christianity and the domestication of the radical gospel of Jesus. To that end, we offer an ecclesially-based critique of the spirituality-at-work movement, the rise of corporate chaplaincy, the religious ministry to capitalist elites, and the do-it-yourself spiritual reengineering of authors like Laurie Beth Jones.

Among the most pernicious aspects of the spirituality-at-work movement is its tendency to further the marginalization of the church as a social structure of importance to Christians. By asserting prerogatives and claiming functions once reserved to the Christian community itself, the corporation feeds the mistaken notion that faith is an individualistic product and quest, in which the body of Christ is at best an option and at worst a deterrent. That the church's own weaknesses and compromise of the gospel has contributed mightily to such marginalization does not detract from the independent damage done by the spirituality-at-work movement.

While the corporate spirituality movement proclaims its independence and distance from historic Christianity, at least in the United States, it nonetheless utilizes, exploits, and trades in a variety of Christian concepts, values, and symbols that have been detached and separated from the contexts of believing communities. Notions of transcendence, vocation, and covenant—which for most people in the United States and many Western capitalist countries make little sense apart from the Christian experience—now exist as free-standing but empty categories, to be filled according to the profit and efficiency strategies of corporate managers. In a sense, the cultural resonance of Christian symbolism and theology survives as a useful "hook" into the hearts and minds of employees in cultures like our own. It is the human relations equivalent of advertising and marketing practices that exploit decontextualized religious images, symbols, and narratives to sell commodities like cars, coffee, and beer. These corporate practices we have labeled "symbolic predators," and have examined elsewhere (Budde, 1997); the spirituality-at-work movement in many of its expressions exhibits a similar exploitation of "meanings" it does not create in order to further non- (and sometimes anti-) Christian objectives.

That most churches contribute to their own social marginality does not make the situation any less lamentable. Instead of asking whether the spirituality-at-work phenomenon offers a rival gospel to that of Christ, the churches too often seek to demonstrate their value to capitalist firms by assisting in workplace spirituality programs. To the extent that it acquiesces in the triumph of a generic spirituality over the particularity of the gospel, the church testifies to its own irrelevance. Why assume the ethic of self-sacrifice and other-regardedness typical of the Christian way when one can be just as "spiritual" (even "Christianly" spiritual) in any number of ways, none of which imposes any obligations, sacrifices, or costs on self-actualizing seekers? Of course, some spirituality at work programs *do* emphasize self-sacrifice and other-regardedness, but only in ways compatible with the sort of self-exploitation needed to keep profits up, unions out, and dissent muzzled. One need not hold to an unyielding form of "no salvation outside the church" to recognize that the elevation of non-specific spirituality (with grand claims to universal applicability and validity) devalues the particularity of the gospel and encourages the worst kind of religious indifferentism—the "I'm OK, you're OK" religiosity that has done so much to rob Christianity of its prophetic heritage in liberal cultures.

As columnist Tom Blackburn notes, the types of "virtues" capitalist firms encourage directly and indirectly—self-discipline, civility, trust, self-command, cosmopolitanism—are not "biblical virtues." Rather,

> They are virtues motivational speakers stress when they earn fees by making audiences feel better about themselves. They are virtues that promote a labor force more eager to work hard for employers. . . .
>
> These character traits masquerading as virtues are the qualities that keep the assembly line moving, the sales force making calls and workers accepting the will of management instead of forming unions. Capitalist virtues make you a reliable citizen. But they are hardly the sum nor the substance of moral life (1995, p. 16).

In contrast, the church is (or should be) about being the new creation, a gathering of disciples that heralds the kingdom of God. As persons made in the image and likeness of God (Gen. 1:26), human beings ought not be formed into tools that serve lesser gods like the firm, but instead the full unfolding of the human person is realized in communion with Christ and the redemption of all creation. The church is meant to be God's social laboratory in the world, a prototype of human community that crosses all the world's divisions and holds together without killing and exploitation as its glue—as such it is meant to prefigure the kingdom of God, not a lean-production capitalist firm in which the few dominate and exploit the many inside and outside the firm.

The spirituality-at-work phenomenon also fuels the instrumentalist orientation toward faith that dominates our cultural environment—this time by encouraging employees to measure the value of spirituality by what it does for them in terms of happiness, self-esteem, work motivation, or career success. That may be an acceptable orientation for some religious traditions, but it is death to the Christianity that looks to Jesus of Nazareth as the exemplar of faith and life. For all of his spiritual maturity and gifts, Jesus produced little of economic value to the powerful, was not known to follow their orders very well, and had a career ladder shaped like a cross. The Jesus described in the Gospel accounts is the *last* type of person firms want their employees to emulate, but he is—or should be—the primary role model for the church.

The churches have mostly recognized the problems produced by allowing the state to control the church (as in direct establishment arrangements)—compromised integrity, lackeyism, an inoffensive and watered-down expression of faith. But insofar as the mainstream churches remain limited by the Constantinian bargain (a measure of institutional freedom in exchange for being useful to and supportive of existing powers and dominant ideologies), they may not even recognize how some versions of the spirituality-at-work phenomenon represent a private-sector version of Constantinianism. Corporations that seek to cater to the "spiritual needs" of their workers do so in the same way that coal mining companies, for example, once built churches for their employees—the company-store way. In both cases, the corporation chooses the ministers, approves the theology, schedules the services, and makes sure that the spirituality on offer reinforces the authority of the boss and the "evils" of worker organization. Company-store theology, whether done crudely or smoothly, cripples the church and preempts the true gospel (with its unpredictability and hostility to coercion) with a controlled and controlling spiritual ideology. For the most part, churches wedded to a Constantinian worldview cannot discern the signs of the times that point to another capture of Christianity by the principalities and powers of our age.

By telling employees that spirituality properly pursued makes for happy corporate functionaries, a wealthy firm, and a stronger nation, corporations further the absorption of Christianity by the capitalist worldview and culture, in the process robbing the church of its prophetic and eschatological qualities. The church falls victim to idolatry on the installment plan. Such a state of affairs does not trouble the corporations—indeed, they profit from such tendencies—but it should trouble the churches more than it does.

The cooperation of the churches in their own marginalization is more evident in the move into corporate chaplaincy programs. Whatever its benefits to individuals, the expansion of corporate chaplaincy is especially troubling as it subordinates church workers to the priorities of the employer. Among other things, chaplaincy often transforms ethical questions—Is what my firm produces morally defensible? Is my prosperity defensible if built upon the exploitation of others?—into therapeutic ones. The questions then become, Why am I having trouble being a team player? Why do I let unproductive guilt inhibit my search for happiness, self-esteem, and the approval of my superiors?

Chaplaincy accepts the assumptions of the institutions in which it operates, and asserts that Christians can support any and all such institutions where Christian chaplains are allowed to practice. The wholesale adoption of corporate chaplaincy threatens to remove capitalism itself from the realm of ethical reflection, dispute, and theological scrutiny. Thus an immensely powerful part of the principalities and powers that dominate the world becomes insulated from the critique of the gospel and the anticipation of the kingdom of God.

Corporate chaplaincy programs are a piece of the velvet glove of lean capitalism—helping to make the painful medicine more palatable, treating the system's victims piecemeal, helping channel employee discontent into isolated personnel matters, and obscuring the conflicts between corporate and employee self-interests with religious pieties and therapy. There will inevitably be a backlash against corporate chaplains and against the church as employees eventually see through the facade of disinterested benevolence to see the face of the same human resources people who "regrettably" must fire them from their job when management's profitability goals so dictate. Business chaplains will eventually come to be regarded with the same degree of contempt that attaches to company doctors and nurses who act more to protect the employer from costly health claims than to protect the health and welfare of workers. When the backlash comes, the church's credibility will suffer from having thrown in with the owners and upper managers rather than the employees.

Chaplaincy inevitably raises the question of divided loyalties—a perennial problem in military chaplaincy (a particularly scandalous example of such conflicts exists in El Salvador, where the Archbishop of San Salvador recently accepted the position as Military Vicar, becoming a commissioned officer over the same army that assassinated one of his predecessors, Archbishop Oscar Romero). To whom are chaplains—military or corporate—ultimately responsible? To their denominational or hierarchical superiors? To their superiors in the military or corporate chain of command? To their contracting agency? Their clients? To God? How are questions of conflict, competing imperatives, and the like to be adjudicated?

The manner in which such questions have been dealt with in the military for centuries—almost always by defining away conflicts or potential role incompatibilities—gives no confidence that such conflicts in a business setting will be handled any differently.

Questions of accountability and loyalty are hard enough when dealing with chaplains having denominational ties. It becomes further muddled when considering lay vs. ordained chaplains and free-agent ministers, some of whom are as much "spiritreneurs" as are Laurie Beth Jones and her associates. There is no reason to suppose, in other words, that corporate chaplains will operate with any greater autonomy or primary loyalty to God or the church than they do in the military or other contexts in which the rules of the game are set by institutions and practices separate from the Christian community.

Top-down chaplaincy programs like the Woodstock Business Conference continue the distortion of pastoral priorities and epistemologies within the church. They continue the elite focus of much theology and social ethics—an economic equivalent of John Howard Yoder's critique of political Constantinianism, which trims the gospel to fit with the sovereign's role and responsibilities in statecraft (thus killing and coercion are made permissible for Christians, but pacifism is not). The measure of Christian social ethics becomes "What sort of religious posture is consistent with the role responsibilities of the CEO and chairman of the board?" Christian executives may derive a good night's sleep for a conscience so assuaged, but they will never be pushed to any sort of significant or world-changing self-scrutiny by the chaplains under contract to them.

When considering the myriad of corporate-sponsored "values" consultants and symposia (e.g., Chopra, Lowe, and others), it is not clear how many (nor how deeply) workers buy into the sorts of corporate spirituality on offer. It might not be too much to wonder if a theological variant of Gresham's Law might be operating here—just as bad or counterfeit money drives down the worth of legitimate currency, so too might the tepid and superficial nature of corporate spirituality diminish the capacity to desire and appreciate more substantive notions of faith, commitment, and vocation.

The whole array of spiritual boosterism proffered by pinstriped shamans, vision questers, rah-rah motivators, and self-promoting authors should be so transparently non-Christian as to make elaboration unnecessary. To the extent that they have recent antecedents in the Christian tradition, they are of the Gospel of Wealth, the Health and Wealth Gospel, and the Godly Prosperity types offered by figures as diverse as Andrew Carnegie, Russell Conway, Jim Bakker, and the Reverend Ike. But as many churches in the United States and Western Europe seek to regain membership and social influence by promising to meet the personal, professional, emotional, and "spiritual" needs of the unattached, they lose their capacity to recognize and critique such non-Christian theologies at work in the larger marketplace. Thus they remain indifferent to—if not actively abetting—the replacement of Christianity as the call-and-response between divine vocation and human response with a "What can you do for me today?" approach that turns the church into a vending machine of material and emotional benefits.

Just as spirituality should not be used as a lever to pry more work and subservience from employees, so is it (from a Christian perspective) inappropriate to use the Christian tradition as a source of uncritical affirmation, consolation, and strategic career enhancement. To the extent that Christianity conveys a legitimate sense of affirmation and consolation to its adherents, it does so as a *by-product* of following the Way of Jesus—a path that cannot avoid the cross en route to the promised kingdom of God. The cheap grace on offer from Laurie Beth Jones and other purveyors of a corporate Christ cannot save humanity from its sinful condition. It cannot lead Christians to their true vocation, to becoming the new community joined not by coercion and power-seeking but by sacrificial self-giving, mutual assistance, and forgiveness as modeled by Jesus. The church as a real, visible alternative society (however imperfectly it lives that mandate) can never accept the false god of *Jesus CEO*, of Bruce Barton's "Jesus-The-Macho-Salesman," or any other for-profit Christ, without mortgaging both its fidelity and its true destiny.

The corporate embrace of spirituality (and the appropriation of specifically Christian categories by some in the business world) is like an acid that corrodes everything it clutches. It simultaneously floods the culture with degraded forms of spiritual and religious engagement and cheapens whatever living religious traditions it ransacks for exploitable ideas, practices, and dispositions. We will return to this appropriation of Christianity by advertising and marketing industries in the next chapter.

The capacity of the church to recognize and combat its own marginalization by outside actors like corporations is diminished, we suggest, by changed ideas and commitments *within* Christian circles. Within the Catholic tradition, one shift among many stands out as particularly troubling—namely, the capitulation to capitalist ideology, economy, and politics exemplified in the 1991 encyclical *Centesimus Annus*. We examine this surrender in chapter 5.

3

The Political Economy of Formation

His image is used to promote cement companies and bakeries, and to sell music CDs, videotapes, t-shirts, hats, mugs, and potato chips. His tours attract corporate sponsors like Federal Express, Mercedez Benz, Kodak, Hewlett Packard, and Pepsi.

We're not talking about Michael Jordan, nor Michael Jackson, nor the reigning pop music or movie idol *du jour,* but about the brave new world of Pope John Paul II, the world's most desirable product endorser. At a time when for-profit culture industries orchestrate human attention to an unprecedented degree, we now witness a strange kind of institutional overlap where religious groups adopt the latest in advertising and marketing techniques and corporations sell their wares by exploiting deeply treasured religious symbols, images, and stories.

Given the stature and aura that still surround the Church and the papacy for many people, it remains jarring to see examples like these:

—To finance the Pope's 1998 visit to Mexico City, the Archdiocese of Mexico City received corporate sponsorship from more than two dozen firms. The single largest sponsor was the Pepsi-owned Sabritas chip company, which paid $1.8 million for the right to use the pope's image in its packaging. The Spanish-language play on words—"Las Papas del Papa" ("The Potatoes of the Pope") was lost on absolutely no one. Equally obvious were the seemingly inescapable TV and billboard ads connecting the pope's picture

with Bimbo bread, a local cement company, and other joint promotions between the church and its corporate benefactors.

—John Paul the multimedia pop star produces cross-media synergy to rival that of any Disney or TimeWarner commodity. His
Holiness has the culture-industry clout to command a $9 million
book advance for *Crossing the Threshold of Hope,* which received
worldwide promotion and simultaneous release in twenty-one
languages and thirty-five countries.

—In 1993, Catholic leaders contracted with Famous Artists
Merchandising Exchange to handle licensing of more than one
hundred products tied to the pope's appearance at World Youth
Day in Denver. Famous Artists promised revenues sufficient to
cover 20 percent of the World Youth Day expenses; given the
firm's experience handling licensing deals for the Rolling Stones,
the Toronto Blue Jays baseball team, Paul McCartney, and others,
the estimates seemed reasonable. Unfortunately, both promoter
and Church officials were disappointed in the final tally, producing lawsuits by the parties against one another. One lesson learned
from the Denver experience, according to officials of the Archdiocese of Newark, was to cut out the middleman when it came
time to market the pope's 1994 visit to Giants Stadium. The Archdiocese handled all licensing and marketing out of its central purchasing office, thus producing a revenue stream free from the
demands of outside partners (Janofsky, 1993; Goldman, 1994).

The Church's embrace of for-profit advertising and marketing
techniques extends beyond the pope-as-pitchman phenomenon.
Ever-expanding areas of ecclesial life, ministry, and outreach utilize the latest in culture-industry techniques and strategies. Consider the following:

—The patrimony of the Church has become a cash cow for the
Vatican, thanks to a variety of joint ventures and promotions. In
one, the Vatican has authorized a line of merchandise "inspired" by
the Vatican Library's collection of more than one million books and
100,000 prints and drawings. These commodities—ranging from
$5,000 rugs, $160 Ferragamo scarves, and four hundred other products—are expected net to the Vatican $5–15 million per year. The
Vatican Library is also of interest to IBM, which pays for the right
to add twenty thousand images per year to the IBM Digital Library.

—In 1999, the Vatican approved a licensing deal with Miami-based Siesta Telecom to issue a Pope John Paul II pre-paid phone card. The card comes with a signed certificate and the pope's likeness on the card; the company already sells phone cards with the Virgin Mary's picture on them. According to Dave Estep, vice president for sales and marketing for Siesta, "Through our business, people will not only be able to buy something that is very useful, but will be gaining a spiritual blessing through the messages sent by the Pope."

—Church leaders now turn to for-profit advertising agencies to recruit new priests and nuns, to encourage fallen-away Catholics to return to the Church, even to carry the message of forgiveness to the world. Market-driven approaches find their way even into religious education programs. As one prominent priest and Catholic educator said, "Educators and parents have to present Jesus' program as a formula for happiness. Christianity doesn't have to make you poverty-stricken or feel guilty for having money or enjoying things" (*US Catholic,* 1994, p. 27).

—Public relations efforts are also integrated into the advertising and marketing strategies of many Church programs and initiatives. The Italian Bishops Conference has wide-ranging contracts with Saatchi and Saatchi, one of the world's pioneers in global advertising, marketing, and public relations. Saatchi and Saatchi now helps the Church in Italy sell papal trinkets and memorabilia, solicit taxpayer support for clergy salaries and overseas relief work, and other projects. In the United Kingdom, the five major Christian churches (including the Catholics and the Church of England) have backed major ad campaigns aimed at boosting Easter worship attendance with appeals that deliberately remove all references to the cross in order to boost the campaign's positive response rate. Keep in mind that, in the British case, churches are prevented from much discussion about God—including statements like "God exists"—because such constitutes an "unsubstantiated claim" prohibited by Independent Television Commission guidelines on advertising. We also have the U.S. Catholic bishops contracting with the public relations giant Hill and Knowlton (the group that helped whip up support for the Gulf War on behalf of the Bush administration in 1990) to revive the Church's sagging antiabortion effort. Finally, witness the tactics of the Papal Foundation Incorporated, a private group that has successfully adapted the sales tactic of premium gifts to the world of Catholic philanthropy— donors of $1 million or more get a nice medallion, a gold pin, a certificate, and a visit with the pope in his private library.

—Not even the physical structures of the Church are beyond the reach of corporate promotion. In October 1999, live television across Europe carried the formal presentation of the refurbished St. Peter's Basilica. The $5 million bill for the two-and-a-half year restoration was paid by a host of corporate sponsors, most notably ENI, the Italian state oil company. Pope John Paul II praised ENI for its "bountiful generosity which made the restoration possible, employing the most modern techniques." This most recent restoration-by-sponsorship continues a precedent set in the 1980s, when a Japanese broadcasting network paid for the restoration of Michaelangelo's ceiling frescoes in the Sistine Chapel (in exchange for high-profile visibility for the firm). Similarly, in 1998 a German appliance manufacturer underwrote the cleaning of Bernini's Collonade at the edge of St. Peter's Square (D'Emilio, 1999).

The puzzlement engendered by the enthusiastic embrace of corporate marketing, public relations, and salesmanship by church groups not known for such is matched by a parallel movement in the world of advertising and marketing. The symbols, images, stories, and songs of religious communities—especially, but not exclusively, of Christianity—inhabit the ads, pitches, and sales appeals of our time in more and more numerous and varied ways.

Here, too, examples are not hard to find. Volvo now claims its cars will "save your soul," MCI uses priests to testify to the reliability of its rate plans, and one particular detergent claims for itself power to wash clean even the Shroud of Turin. Gatorade has built an entire theology—maybe even a new religion—around the persona of His Airness (maybe it should be His Holiness), Michael Jordan. Whether he's running up Tibetan mountains in search of a remote holy man, or posed in print ads beneath a back-lit basketball rim that puts a halo over his head (the caption there is "for some, heaven is only ten feet up"), this living icon moves with ease between athletic, social, and religious forms of veneration. And in perhaps the most succinct statement of commercial theology, Mercedes Benz promises a litany of blessings and ends up with the slogan, "Sacrifice Nothing."

Recently, one of us received a direct-mail pitch for a VISA credit card "that celebrates your CHRISTIAN FAITH." In fact, the whole appeal reads like an unending festival—the packaging, pitch letter, and enclosures promise to "celebrate" our Christianity no less than nine times, while also promising to "witness" to or "reflect" our faith another three times. The only tie to anything remotely Christian in this loyalty card—besides all that celebrating and witnessing, of course—is the pledge by Capital One, Inc., to devote one-quarter of 1 percent of our charges to the Christian Children's Fund. At that rate, we have to indulge our gluttony, avarice, and greed to the tune of $40,000 in order to send $100 to Sally Struthers's favorite television charity. Of course, we'll be witnessing to and celebrating our CHRISTIAN FAITH quite a bit in the course of running up a $40,000 credit card bill, so there are additional benefits all around.

The appropriation of religious resources also proceeds apace in European culture industries. The *Times* of London advertised itself via a photograph of a crucified Racquel Welch, Volkswagen in France used Jesus at the Last Supper to celebrate the arrival of the new Golf auto model, and a Hungarian television station used pictures of Pope John Paul II to boost viewership.

This strange convergence—traditional churches embracing advertising/marketing techniques and ideologies, and marketers eager to utilize Christianity to sell goods, services, lifestyles, and attitudes—begs for explanation. From the ecclesial side, the embrace of marketing flows from a variety of church weaknesses; for the advertisers, religious symbols and metaphors represent yet another cultural resource to be mined and exploited until no longer useful. For both, the object of the game is formation.

The Politics of Contested Formation

We need to consider briefly in what sense the Christian churches exercise "power" in contemporary times. It has been a long time since churches exercised military power to get their way in the world. The economic power of the Catholic Church is mostly an illusion; it is dwarfed by institutional investors, transnational corporations, currency speculators, and governments. And even a sideways glance at the policies of sovereign states reveals that governments ignore church positions on war, economics, and social policy with few repercussions.

To the extent that the churches influence world events anymore, they do so as a cultural power. The extent to which the church makes the stories of Jesus come alive in human hearts and imaginations, the extent to which Christianity's stories, songs, and symbols mold one's way of being in the world—to that extent does the church move in, for and against other actors and processes in the world.

This process of shaping the habits, affections, and dispositions of people—when it is done by the Christian tradition—is called formation. It is a communal process similar to a craft apprenticeship, in which newcomers learn the explicit and tacit knowledge of practitioners by a process of imitation, then internalization, then innovation. Over time, if formation is successful, newcomers themselves become adept in encountering, imagining, and reasoning through Christian eyes, minds, and hearts. Christian practices of liturgy, religious education, prayer, and action are simultaneously practices of faith formation and products of communities themselves formed by the narratives, symbols, and examples of Jesus and his followers.

Stressing the centrality of formation in Christianity underscores two important points: that Christianity depends on collective, intensive practices distinct from the non-Christian world for its perpetuation; and that the process of "making Christians" is always a precarious matter, which can be undermined or diluted by other powerful institutions and processes of "formation." Consequently, formation is always intrinsically political, whether or not it is recognized as such. It requires institutional agents capable of inculcating their dispositions into human hearts and minds, often in opposition to actors attempting to do the same with different, sometimes conflicting, stories and symbols. How people are formed by cultural processes and actors shapes how they will encounter and react to "experience"; it even affects the capacity to have certain kinds of experience. Some kinds of experiences are unavailable to persons whose language lacks adequate nuance and depth in certain areas. Similarly, the "same" phenomena may, when apprehended by groups with different cultural and linguistic resources, produce different "experiences." It is not simply that different formative processes give people different *interpretations* of experience; rather, some experiences require certain formative prerequisites and resources in order for people to "have" the experience at all.

To be a people capable of loving its enemies, turning the other cheek, or seeing the inbreaking of the promised kingdom of God in the body of a crucified political enemy of the Roman Empire requires a most peculiar kind of formation. In every time and place, the church has formed a people capable of hearing and responding to the gospel of Jesus, the witness of the saints and martyrs, and the challenges of the prophets. Where formation has been neglected, undermined, or done poorly, evidence of such inadequacies appears as pathologies in the body of Christ and its practices, priorities, and affections.

This, then, is the primary sense in which the church is a "cultural" actor and user of cultural power. But it is not the only such actor—indeed, in our time and place, the church is far from being the most powerful cultural actor. In the world made by contemporary capitalism, thousands of for-profit firms of considerable wealth and power are vitally concerned with forming human affections, dispositions, desires, and practices. Capitalism, no less than Christianity, depends on formation processes to sustain itself in the world; making people "fit for capitalism" is no less important to the workings of the world economy than processes of production, distribution, and finance.

Our primary assertion is this: to the extent that capitalist formation succeeds, Christian formation fails. Indeed, it may be on the battleground of formation that the entanglements of church and corporation—and the blending of the two that is part and parcel of Christianity Incorporated—play themselves out most significantly in our time and place. Despite their centuries of experience in matters of human formation, mainstream Protestant and

Catholic churches are losing a contest most aren't aware of having entered.

Developing this point requires that we examine the role of culture and culture industries—and formation as a primary category therein—in contemporary capitalism. Next, we must explore the status of formation in contemporary Christianity in order to assess the intraecclesial strengths and weaknesses of church identity formation and mission. Finally, we must explore how for-profit culture industries undermine processes of Christian formation and the reactive strategies—many of them disastrous—pursued by churches attempting to beat culture industries at their own game. Only then will the full implications of our previous examples of church-as-marketer and marketers-as-spiritualizers be apparent.

Capitalism, Culture, and Formation

Arguing that capitalism of necessity involves processes of formation is to violate several intellectual and conventional assumptions. It stands opposed to many major traditions in political economy (liberal, realist, many variants of Marxism) in which cultural matters are unimportant, derivative of more fundamental processes, or used to explain whatever minor remainders cannot be accounted for by supposedly more robust factors. It also undercuts many of the "theologies of democratic capitalism" produced by Michael Novak (1982) and others, and reflected in Pope John Paul II's encyclical *Centesimus Annus* (1991). In this construct, a key assumption holds that the political, economic, and moral/cultural "systems" of society can be thought of as more or less independent of one another, which allows Novak and his colleagues to attribute the negative aspects of capitalist life to the political and/or moral/cultural systems, but never to the economic system itself. When culture is seen as inseparable from, and oftentimes "produced" by, capitalism as an economic "system," the separate-spheres argument is revealed to be a shell game that keeps moving criticism of capitalism away from economics to the ill-conceived interventionism of states and to cultures with the "wrong" values and priorities.

Defining what constitutes the culture industries today is more challenging than when Max Horkheimer and Theodor Adorno used the term in 1944. Then as now, it includes the means of mass communication—radio, newspapers, popular music, and film, now expanded to include television, home entertainment, video-game software, and the like. These days the culture industry category reaches beyond content providers to include distribution systems (e.g., cable and satellite systems, telecommunications firms, the Internet) and data manipulation firms (software and computer interests, market research firms, and more). While determining the outer boundaries of the culture industries is a matter of some dispute, what is harder to dispute is that the sector is disproportionately influential in the overall operations of contemporary capitalism.

That influence, we suggest, is not due to the sheer size of the cultural sector—indeed, when compared with the automotive, chemical, or agricultural areas of capitalism, firms that buy and sell "culture" seem rather small in comparison. What makes culture industries so important is their strategic position in contemporary capitalism—what firms in these sectors do ultimately affects the fortunes of many other industries, enterprises, and capitalist processes. And what these firms do best, we suggest, is trade in dreams, desires, images, and roles—the stuff of which all kinds of formation (including Christian varieties) is made.

Elsewhere we have provided a longer treatment of culture industries in contemporary capitalism (see Budde, 1997). Here we need only recall that transnational corporations (e.g., Disney, Murdoch's NewsCorp, and AOL Time Warner) control ever-expanding amounts of cultural production: these culture industries are increasingly combined in webs of cross-promotion and "synergy" (for example, a Disney movie spawns a Disney-published book and a Disney-published soundtrack, all of which are hyped on Disney-owned television and radio networks, and which enjoy cross-promotions via Disney's long-term deal with McDonald's restaurants). Deregulation and privatization in cultural sectors worldwide have made advertising the dominant funding base for many culture industries, steadily eclipsing public service, nonprofit, or subsidized regimes (albeit at different rates of change; see generally McChesney, 1998).

These changes are both a cause and consequence of the much discussed "globalization" of contemporary capitalism. While scholars and policy makers debate whether, in fact, globalization is something new under the capitalist sun or merely a new variant on an old tune, culture industries are more important to the overall system than ever before. They are more important because formation is more important than ever in the rapid-production, rapid-turnover, rapid-replacement world of global capitalism.

For several decades, capitalism has had to contend with the problem of overproduction and underconsumption. If people don't buy enough of what is produced (and at a price high enough to secure profits for owners), the whole machine grinds to a halt. Competition between firms has led to more productive firms, more products available for consumption, and increased commodification of activities and endeavors that were previously outside the market matrix. The modern advertising industry arose in the early twentieth century as a way to help firms contend with the so-called "realization problem" in wealthy capitalist countries—in other words, firms don't "realize" a profit, no matter how good or plentiful the stuff they make, until someone buys the stuff. Radio, and later television, became marketing conduits when advertising became their main source of financing—programs became the bait used to draw audiences toward the advertisers' pitch. As culture industries expanded, conglomerated, and globalized in the latter half of the twentieth century, their marketing functions—selling themselves, selling for others, and selling particular notions of value—have become more significant, and it is in their marketing functions that the formative powers of culture industries are most readily apparent (although they do not end there).

When one looks at culture industries as a whole, two functions in particular stand out: the saturation of advanced industrial regimes by the products and presence of these industries, and the degree to which the functions of advertising and marketing permeate all for-profit cultural producers, their processes, and their products. Together these make culture industries a potent formative presence in increasingly expanding areas of the world (McChesney, 1998, p. 4).

Regarding this first point, we in the United States have become so numbed to the presence of corporate image-making that time-and-use statistics no longer startle us. Television watching in the United States and Japan (Western European figures are rising along with the increased number of television stations there) consumes more waking hours than all activities except working for money (Murray-Brown, 1991, p. 19). Young people watch twenty to twenty-five hours of television per week, and listen to the radio several more hours per day (Ekstrom, 1992). The average child will have spent between 19,000 and 24,000 hours in school if he or she does not drop out before completing high school (the equivalent of between 2.1 and 2.7 full years of one's life; see Ekstrom, 1992, p. 135); in comparison, over the course of a seventy-five-year lifespan, nearly thirteen years of an average American's life will be spent watching television—three full years of which will have been commercials (Jacobson and Mazur, 1995, p. 41). Even if viewers are not attentive to television and other cultural products at all times, their overall involvement remains enormous.

A major study on youth and media appeared in late 1999, funded by the prestigious Kaiser Family Foundation (Roberts et al., 1999). Unlike many other studies, this one explored both media *use* (how many hours per day attentively involved with a single cultural product) and media *exposure* (the total amount of media product encountered per day). Because many people use two or more forms of media at once (e.g., listening to the radio while reading a magazine, having the television on while using the Internet), total media exposure is often larger than their daily use—a previously neglected insight.

The numbers produced by the Roberts study suggest patterns of media use and exposure that crowd out most other formative influences in the lives of young people. Overall, children aged two to eighteen average five and a half hours per day of media use, with kids in the eight to thirteen bracket spending more time with media (nearly seven hours per day) than with any other waking activity including school. Multiple use of media (media exposure) means that the five and a half hours of media use translates into six and a half hours of exposure to media content per day; that average hides the large numbers of heavy users, specifically the 30 percent of all children who are exposed to more than seven hours of media product per day. While there are age-specific features of media exposure (kids eight to thirteen are exposed to more than eight hours of product per day, while adolescents fourteen to eighteen average seven and a half), lifelong exposure begins at a young age (children age two to four average more than four hours of media product exposure per day) (Roberts, 1999).

The percentage of people who voluntarily remove themselves from high-volume consumption of culture industry products is quite small: only 5 percent of children report less than one hour per day with culture industries (Roberts, 1999, p. 18). According to the Roberts study, the "average" U.S. household environment includes three televisions, two VCRS, three radios, three tape players, two CD players, a video game player, and a computer (only the last item shows substantial variation in unit ownership by income and other factors). More U.S. households have televisions than have flush toilets. Even for those seeking to avoid high-volume involvement with culture industries, the presence of the industries and their products is nearly inescapable.

One expert estimates that Americans are exposed to ads, logos, brand identifiers, jingles, and other forms of corporate symbolic expression at the rate of sixteen thousand per day (Savan, 1994, p. 1). Even for those who "just say no" to one component of the culture industry matrix—those who don't watch television, for example—the cultural ecology in which they live is dominated by newspapers, magazines, radio, direct mail, and billboards, all of which are plugged into television and the culture it creates. In other words, the lived environment of advanced industrial countries (and increasingly, most other parts of the world) is flooded with the songs, symbols, and stories produced by the likes of Time Warner, Murdoch, Disney, Viacom, and Sony. Their density, the saturation exposures they enjoy, and their undeniable appeal make them inescapable, unavoidable, and powerful as institutional actors that exert a formative influence on human emotions, imaginations, and dispositions.

The second point—the centrality of advertising and marketing to all culture industries—represents the triumph of the U.S. for-profit model of cultural finance over alternatives of public service, tax-supported, and noncommercial cultural production. This triumph represents the successful imposition of neoliberal policies of deregulation and privatization worldwide through institutions like the International Monetary Fund and the World Trade Organization. These multilateral agencies, dominated by the U.S. government (whose cultural policy in turn reflects the priorities of the largest for-profit culture industries) have steadily worn down trade barriers, public subsidies, and other alternatives to marketing- and advertising-driven cultural production. While noncommercial cultural products and institutions endure, they continue to lose ground in the competition for public time and attention to those whose utility as sales vectors is more pronounced. Given the desire of commercial advertisers to put audiences in a relaxed, distress-free mode conducive to sales pitches (documentaries on starvation in Africa do little to put people in a receptive mood for luxury cars, in this view), entertainment formats continue to be preferred by those who sponsor television and other mass media (see Herman and Chomsky, 1988).

Both together and separately, television and advertising/marketing represent two of the most powerful means of human formation in our world. If we are to gauge adequately the degree of conflict between capitalist and Christian formation, we must look at how the world of commerce and the world of faith shape human affections, dispositions, and practices; doing so will illustrate the extent to which the formative practices of for-profit culture industries triumph over the cultivation of Christian ways of being in the world.

The Velvet Glove of Capitalist Power: Advertising, Marketing, and Desire

Repetition and association constitute key aspects of the formative power of for-profit culture industries. Repetition is assured in a culture like our own which is saturated by the images, songs, stories, and commercial appeals of the culture industries. Association—a process that ties cultural products to emotional, affective, and normative qualities—is a complex and oftentimes unpredictable interaction between audiences, institutional factors, and cultural products. The formative powers of association are most clear in examining the theory and practice of contemporary advertising and marketing. This examination, however, requires first that we take notice of several contextual considerations.

First, the cultural environment of contemporary capitalism is unlike any that has ever existed. Exposure to mediated messages and experiences is more voluminous, more continuous, and more pervasive than ever before. Advertising messages in particular are everywhere, serving as round-the-clock backgrounds to our daily lives. They are in all environments, from grocery stores and hospitals to bedrooms and churches. The output of other culture industries—movies, television, music videos, and recorded music—adds further to the unprecedented commercial and symbolic saturation of life in contemporary capitalism.

The sheer volume, diversity, and impermanence of cultural production have largely broken ties between symbols and that to which they refer, a phenomenon known as fragmentation (Jameson, 1991, pp. 26–27; Firat, 1991, p. 71). Symbols can no longer be assumed to have a constant, more-or-less commonly understood relationship to some independent, "real" referent; rather, symbols in commercial culture are constantly recombined, reshuffled, and replaced with an eye toward attaching novel "meanings" to various products and consumption opportunities (Firat, 1991). "Meaning," in such a world, is constructed from a goulash of symbols, narratives, and prior "meanings" in play in the cultural environment; any given symbol is likely to have "polyvalent meaning," a multitude of different meanings depending on how it is appropriated by different subgroups within an audience. These detached symbols and clusters of meaning are aligned, paired, or similarly "transferred" to consumption opportunities by marketers and others who must generate demand adequate for profitability and thus the healthy functioning of the economy.

Second, the nature of advertising appeals has shifted substantially since the industry's earliest days. Leiss, Klein, and Jhally

(1990) are among those who have documented the shift in message appeals from utilitarian, product-focused ads toward buyer-centered, image-related approaches that now dominate contemporary advertising. Nowadays, advertising campaigns "generally do not present logical arguments and claims for their products. Instead, they seek to associate their product with evocative images and themes" (Strate, 1991, p. 113). Advertising discourse and practice in so-called postmodern culture, according to critics and practitioners alike, are infused with myth, narrative, symbolism, and the raw materials of nonmarket cultural codes, traditions, and meanings. One marketer talks of creating an emotional bond between consumers and a product brand, of "creating mythologies about their brands by humanizing them and giving them distinct personalities and cultural sensibilities" (*Marketing News*, February 17, 1992, p. 19).

In such a context—a media-saturated environment with ceaseless, meaning-laden market appeals—a revised epistemological approach is needed for analysis and action. In earlier times, when the commercialization of everyday life was less thorough, media studies focused on the "effects" of individual messages, ads, or programs (see Verbeke, 1992, p. 1; Harvey, 1989, p. 287; Mattelart, 1991, p. 213). In the contemporary situation, in which the *flow* (unceasing, reinforcing, in multiple media) of commercial, mediated symbols is the dominant reality, concentrating on single messages or ads seems unjustifiably narrow. Whatever effects derive from commercial culture, such can only be effects of the total flow—and the significance of any single item in that flow can be ascertained only in relation to other items in that flow over time (see Shanahan and Morgan, 1999). When one moves beyond the model of media or advertising "effects" literature ("Does a one-time Pepsi ad make people buy Pepsi?") it becomes possible to see how advertising and marketing act as powerful formative agents.

Whether one looks at television, advertising, or other culture industries, attitudinal and affective formation is more likely to act slowly and powerfully rather than quickly and weakly (the general point made about television by Shanahan and Morgan, 1999, p. 55). Consider, for example, how the aforementioned shift in twentieth-century advertising theory and practice—from product-centered to consumer-centered—has increased the role of information in advertising. Knowledge about consumers has become a prized commodity; it affects not only all aspects of sales and marketing, but many other aspects of corporate strategy.

Advanced capitalist countries are so thoroughly scrutinized by commercial interests—which gather and utilize information on births, deaths, ages, occupational histories, weddings, race and ethnicity, credit histories, illnesses, hobbies, cultural heroes, sexual behaviors, and countless other things—that it is easy to forget how truly radical, one-way, and basic to our social environment are such information-gathering and -utilizing practices. Traditional demographic categories have long been an important aspect of information collection and observation; in the contemporary context, these are joined to new types of information and knowledge about consumers. Many of these new sorts of knowledge focus on subconscious or nonrational phenomena. Giving the lie to notions of consumer sovereignty and rationality, various programs of psychographic research continue searching for emotional, precognitive, and value-based "triggers" that can be grasped in efforts to generate consumption-oriented behaviors (see Piirto, 1991 for a business-oriented history of psychographic research; see also Kamakure and Novak, 1992, and Goerne, 1992, for examples). Those words, concepts, pictures, sounds, and other components that "resonate" favorably among various segments of mass markets (determined by extensive testing and research) becomes the stuff of modern ad appeals (e.g., Piirto, 1991, pp. 90–91). Sophisticated psychological testing continues to search for knowledge about people unknown to the individuals themselves and for reliable advertising strategies capable of translating that knowledge into corporate-desired behaviors and attitudes (Piirto, 1991, p. 14, 126–28; Goerne, 1992, p. H–32). In this regard, according to Oscar Gandy Jr., "every day thousands of U.S. consumers participate in [market and psychological] experiments without the benefit of having any informed consent forms" (1993, p. 68). While largely developed in the United States, such research approaches are increasingly utilized on a global scale (Piirto, 1991, pp. 142–66; *Marketing News,* Aug. 26, 1987; Marriott, 1986).

Marketing—as an institution generating powerful knowledge—operates increasingly as a fully coherent system, constantly integrating feedback (performance and outcome data, unanticipated effects, the impact and experiences of other marketers) into new strategies and research. Information about potential customers is generated from seemingly limitless sources—from credit card transactions to hidden cameras in supermarkets used to observe consumer responses to various display, position, price, and other variables.

A routine trip to an American supermarket subjects people to a controlled environment in which variations in architecture and layout, background music and scents, lighting and temperature are tested, assessed, and assembled to shape consumer behavior and dispositions in ways that fly below the radar of conscious awareness. The immense knowledge-generating potential of bar-coded data gathering systems ("scanner" technology in multiple forms) is only now becoming apparent and is becoming a pervasive feature of advanced capitalist societies.

According to Gandy,

> The importance of the development of scanner technology cannot be overstated. Scanning from point-of-purchase terminals, such as the checkout counter in the supermarket, provides data at high speed and in real time about the status of the market as well as the responsiveness of consumers to variations in price and representation. . . . But the scanning technology also provides the organization with the option of gathering this information at the level of purchases by identified individuals. Special mailings or other distributions of promotional materials to persons whose identities are scanned at the time they pay for their purchases facilitates the linkage between inventory control and marketing central to the emerging just-in-time approach to manufacturing, which links production to consumption (1993, p. 66).

In other words, millions of consumers trade lower prices on grocery and other purchases for personal information that corporations can then use to sell these same people a variety of products more effectively—even products these consumers didn't realize they might "need" or want until targeted by these customized sales efforts.

One such way that advertising/marketing utilizes the power of information is through the commonplace techniques of "associative advertising" (summarized by Waide, 1987, pp. 73–74). It involves, among other things, the following characteristics:

—Advertising strategies that identify a "deep-seated nonmarket good for which people in the target market feel a strong desire." Such a good is one which cannot by definition be bought and sold in markets (for example friendship, acceptance, and esteem). In most cases the marketed product "bears only the most tenuous (if any) relation to the nonmarket good with which it is associated in the advertising campaign. For example, soft drinks cannot give one friends, sex, or excitement."

—"If possible, the desire for the nonmarket good is intensified by calling into question one's acceptability." Advertising associates the product with a nonmarket value it cannot possibly satisfy, while stimulating feelings of personal inadequacy and anxiety.

—The satisfaction of the nonmarket value exploited by associative advertising is partial at best and is usually due to advertising's cultural impact.

> For example, mouthwash has little prolonged effect on stinking breath, but it helps to reduce the intense anxieties reinforced by mouthwash commercials on television because we at least feel that we are doing the proper thing. In the most effective cases of associative advertising, people begin to talk like ad copy. We begin to sneer at those who own the wrong things. We all become enforcers for the advertisers. In general, if the advertising images are effective enough and reach enough people, even preposterous marketing claims can become at least partially self-fulfilling (Waide, 1987, pp. 3–4).

The possible combinations of images and products in a postmodern culture are nearly limitless—associations can change over time to exploit perceived opportunities, and marketers can appropriate new codes developed within subcultures (e.g., punk fashions). With no strong ties between images and referents, and with constant demands to accelerate product turnover and purchasing, advertising has come to assume "a much greater role in the growth dynamics of capitalism" (Harvey, 1989, p. 287).

In the many ways that advertising/marketing acts to shape human dispositions, desires, and affections—its power of formation, in other words—there is nothing that corresponds to old-fashioned notions of advertising acting "subliminally" or in a "hypodermic" fashion that implants ideas and desires into the minds of countless passive individuals. Nor should one assume that people are stupid, easily duped, or incapable of choice. In fact, the dynamic is more like a seduction than an assault. It involves actor A knowing things about B that B doesn't realize A knows. It is like playing poker against someone who has already seen your hand, unbeknownst to you, in a blurred mirror. In such a context, the actor under surveillance chooses, she is acting freely, but she does so in a context constructed to advance the priorities of others. So long as the one-sidedness in information persists, and so long as the player under surveillance is unaware of the degree of contextual manipulation and structuring, the manipulative interaction can continue indefinitely. And the fact that the surveillance is imperfect (it cannot accurately connect with resonant symbols, etc., every time) only adds to the illusion of an interaction among free, equal parties, insofar as not all advertising "works"; just as peeking at another's poker hand via a blurred mirror provides a less than perfect picture of another's cards. Human desires, notions of beauty, insecurities, etc., are both exploited and shaped by the nonstop, inescapable, and information-driven nature of contemporary advertising and marketing.

However, from a corporate perspective, the power of capitalist formation has created a new set of problems. Consumers are surrounded by so many pitches, appeals, amusements, and cultural products that it becomes increasingly difficult for any single message to stand out. Finding cultural resources that one can "associate" effectively with products and sponsors becomes more difficult as overexposure dilutes the affective power of cultural resources already in play—once a song has become fixed to a product (the Motown hit "Heard It Through the Grapevine" with the

California Raisins, for example), it becomes quite difficult to use that same song to create a positive disposition for another unrelated product.

Consequently, practitioners of corporate formation and advertising must continually find new raw cultural material, previously ignored or explored deposits of meaning and significance—the cultural equivalent of slash-and-burn agriculture, if you will. While overt Christian symbols and images have long been considered mostly off-limits for respectable advertisers, such reticence is now an outdated inhibition to be overcome in the search for new yet familiar sorts of ad appeals and campaigns. Firms now exploit Christianity to sell everything from luxury cars to long-distance telephone service to computer operating systems because they see in many Western cultures a broad but not deep reservoir of stories, images, and metaphors that are familiar enough to connect with audiences, but not so deeply internalized by (or important to) them as to cause much beyond token opposition.

As media scholar Lynn Clark notes, "The symbols [of Christianity] are up for grabs, to be used by anyone who wants" (Charry, 1997). Marketers of all sorts are grabbing those symbols, according to business journalist Jennifer Harrison, who notes "More and more ads are drawing on the rich possibilities of religious and spiritual themes and schemes. From cars to beverages, and health care to sports teams, we see signs and portents that Madison Avenue has jumped on the spiritual bandwagon" (*American Demographics*, 1997). A government agency in Great Britain notes that, while in years past religion was exploited in advertising only during the Christmas season, it is now deployed year-round (Boshoff, 1998, p. 5). That this utilization is broader—using religious symbols and metaphors of many (often vague) sorts, suggests that the exploitation of spiritual and Christian resources is an increasingly prevalent practice.

Ironically, the corporate raid on Christianity, in which marketers become "symbolic predators" that exploit and drain the Christian symbolic universe of its power and intelligibility, would have been impossible without the churches' prior formation of human attitudes and practices. The corporate expropriation of Christian cultural capital comes roughly at the same time that the formative capacities of the churches themselves have become mostly moribund, ineffective, and increasingly desperate. It is this desperation that moves the uncritical rush to "market the faith" by mainstream churches, a move that requires more sustained attention to Christian formation in a capitalist cultural ecology.

Christian Formation in the Media Flood

As mentioned previously, there is nothing natural or innate about being a Christian (or a Jew, or a surgeon, or a stamp collector). Being a Christian is an identity that one acquires from others—a set of dispositions, affections, and practices that are learned from persons already formed by the narratives, songs, and traditions of the faith. Becoming a Christian is like learning a trade or a foreign language—it requires disciplined apprenticeship under the guidance of others who have internalized the competencies, nuances, and satisfactions attendant to a trade done well or a language rendered eloquently.

The process of forming Christians has never been automatic, easy, or flawless. In the cultural ecology of contemporary capitalism—with its nonstop flow of images, symbols, sounds, and attractions—Christian formation faces daunting new obstacles that most church leaders scarcely acknowledge. Because most seek to be full participants in American capitalism and society, in which radical or structural critique is considered beyond the bounds of "constructive engagement," church leaders are too often reduced to inconsequential hand-wringing about media sex and violence, and yuletide clichés about consumerism.

The unpleasant truth is that, for mainstream congregations of Catholics and Protestants, formation is an underfunded, neglected, and often token exercise. What is called formation usually focuses on children more than adults (usually ending in the teen years), proffers an individualistic notion of Christianity, and is thoroughly at home in a world in which it is understood that more powerful loyalties—to the state, to middle-class aspirations, to the ideology of capitalism—must be respected and accommodated.

The capacity to form anything more than shallow Christianity—the sort of identity that one puts on or takes off as circumstances dictate but that never orders or controls other allegiances—requires significant amounts of time, effort, and social space free from the dictates of the dominant culture. None of these are present in most of the Christian formation efforts that touch Catholics (and many Protestants) in the United States. Fewer than 5 percent of all U.S. Catholics invest as much time per *month* in church-related activism, study, or involvement (beyond Mass attendance) as American Catholics invest per *week* in the company of their television (see Castelli and Gremillion, 1987, p. 67). In the course of a year, most American Catholics will read no books about their faith (past or present, or its spiritual or social legacy), subscribe to no Christian newspaper or magazine—will do nothing, in other words, to broaden or deepen an adult appropriation of their faith tradition. Compare trivial investments of time in matters Christian with the enormous dedication of time, attention, and receptivity to the products of corporate culture industries (movies, advertising and marketing, television, etc.), and there is no question whose formative processes are more effective and deeply rooted in the attitudes, desires, and dispositions of most American Christians (Catholic and Protestant). The intellectual challenge is not in explaining *why* Christian formation loses out to that of capitalist culture, but why anyone would expect any other outcome.

As noted by Marcel Dumestre of the Institute for Ministry at Loyola University in New Orleans,

> As a whole, Catholics do not know their religious heritage. Adult Catholics tend to operate with information about their religion that was gained in their childhood and teen-age years. Typically, Catholic adults have expanded their knowledge base in other areas of their lives, except for their religion (1993, p. 24).

It is easy to condemn a lack of "knowledge about" one's Christian heritage—a circumstance Dumestre says is not new in church history—but we believe at root the problem is more one of religious *fluency* rather than religious *literacy* or fact-acquisition. The need is not simply for knowledge about Christianity, but knowing how to think, feel, and desire as someone formed by and fluent in the stories, symbols, and exemplars of the Christian drama.

While some observers are encouraged by what they see in Christian formation (see Orsi, 1994, p. 394; Gibeau, 1994), we are persuaded that religious formation and education remains a low priority in mainstream U.S. Catholicism. As noted by Anne Marie Mongovern (1992, pp. 234–39) and others, diocesan and parish budget cuts fall first and hardest on religious education, and volunteer staff often lack adequate training or education for their responsibilities. The main program for Catholic children in secular schools (at its height, the Catholic school system never educated more than about one-third of Catholic children in the United States) is the Confraternity of Christian Doctrine (CCD) program. This effort has long been typified by inadequate support and resources, high rates of nonparticipation or token involvement, and uneven levels of staff competence and morale. One veteran CCD teacher agrees with her students that the program is "a waste of time," and should be renamed the "Central City Dump" (CCD) program (Denman, 1992, p. 210). Adult programs fare little better, inasmuch as a typical adult religious education or formation program "tends to be the least systematic and most underfunded parish or school program . . . even the term adult religious education is [now] a turnoff for many people" (Dumestre, 1993, p. 27).

When the early church recognized a non-Christian cultural ecology for what it was—suffused with the imperial pretentions and domesticated deities of Rome—it saw formation as a matter of great seriousness. While not practiced uniformly throughout the Christian diaspora, the Christian catechumenate made—by our diluted contemporary standards—outrageous demands on persons wishing to be Christians. Becoming a Christian meant making discipleship and the body of Christ one's prime identity and allegiance—circumscribing and sometimes abrogating the rival claims of family, profession, and sovereign. The changes required in one's life—how one earned a living, with whom one associated, what one considered desirable or valued—required a long period of apprenticeship (often three years) under more mature adult Christians whose advanced formation was itself ongoing. The profound mysteries of faith—that one could love enemies, that Jesus could be fully present in the eucharistic meal, that neither Caesar nor the sword had the final word in God's redemptive plan—were things novices could not appreciate unless and until they had passed through prerequisite changes in attitude, lifestyle, and commitment (newcomers were typically allowed to hear the liturgy of the word in early worship services, but were required to leave before the Eucharist). Even after several years of learning the language of faith, some candidates for full membership in the *ecclesia* were turned away; unless formation was sufficiently deep and rooted, one could not think, feel, pray, or desire as God intended for members of his new form of human association on earth—namely, the church.

The transformation of Christianity from a marginal community—usually ignored but occasionally persecuted—to the official religion of the Empire pushed the church away from intensive one-on-one formation of persons for whom becoming a Christian was a matter of great consequence and risk. With large numbers of people suddenly seeking church membership—many saw it as a way to curry favor in the imperial system—formation become more routinized, faster, and less discriminating. Additionally, the church watered down its previous understanding of the gospel; the almost-complete presumption of incompatibility between the Way of the Cross and the way of the sword that pertained prior to the fourth century was clearly impractical now that the Emperor himself was the patron of the church. It remained for Augustine to systematize and justify the emerging accommodation between Christianity and the killing necessary for the church to serve adequately as the spiritual support for an empire in decline. Chaplaincy, after all, requires accepting the role requirements of those whom one seeks to succor and support.

The point is not to imitate every particular of the formation practices of the early church. Rather, those of us seeking to "sing the Lord's song in a foreign land" (Ps. 137 RSV) dominated by powerful economic actors seeking to shape and form us in our very depths must recognize that formation must become a central passion if we are to forge a Christianity worthy of the name. Absent such passion, church leaders will likely seek to maintain their social position by adopting an even more diluted ecclesiology that is loathe to offend nominal Christians who are more deeply formed by the state, market, and culture industries. These same leaders are also likely to increase their reliance on the techniques and tactics of the culture industries (especially advertising and marketing) as they attempt to substitute capital-intensive formation for time- and people-intensive approaches centered in a vital and engaging church life. The latter seems unlikely to excite people already deeply formed by spectacle, entertainment, and customized sales pitches; better to rely on slicker media promotions, ad appeals, and market research to add some Christian gloss to the cultural formation one has already judged to be largely congruent with the "essence" of Christianity. Having adopted a supportive posture toward existing relations of power—a chaplaincy posture—conflicts between the formative processes of that culture and those of the church must be minimized or reduced to a concern for secondary details (e.g., "too much sex and violence on television").

Some of the negative ecclesial consequences of the churches' adoption of culture industry practices will likely require many years to manifest themselves. Others are more readily apparent—and however they differ, they all stand both as cause and consequence of the failure of most churches to acknowledge the countercultural potential within Christianity.

For example, the transformation of lay Christians—whose baptism into the church gives them an essential, active, and dramatic share of God's mission on earth—into "consumers" and "customers" is appearing in denominational and freestanding churches alike. Kim Wilson, a church marketing consultant in Atlanta, boasts that her company's efforts "help churches increase attendance by utilizing proven customer service techniques that produce successful companies." A California-based firm uses demographic and target-market research to help churches tailor their ministries and message to the "needs and unique preferences" of persons in their target market (Long, 1997, p. 39).

One should not think that such instrumentalist repositioning of church mission is limited to entrepreneurial megachurches or what British wags call "the happy-clappy faction" of born-again congregations. In fact, the Church of England, stung by dramatic declines in worship attendance, social stature, and the efficacy of its means of ecclesial formation, is among the most aggressive promoters of market research, public relations, and ad campaigns.

Dr. Bill Beavers, director of communications for the Church of England, defends the choice to look at church members as "customers." Not only will the church itself benefit from the use of corporate market research to identify ways to meet customer needs and desires, so will Great Britain as a whole. "If we are going to make a contribution to the nation," said Beavers in pitching the value of chaplaincy from a fading state church, "the Church has to be more businesslike" (Combe, 1999).

The Anglican Church, both on its own and in cooperation with other major churches in the United Kingdom (including Catholic and Methodist), has sponsored several mass media ad campaigns with top-quality production values, wealthy and attractive models and celebrities, and hip music scores. One diocesan communications director admits that "there will be people who say we are prostituting ourselves by trying to sell the Church," but such is necessary inasmuch as "We want to move away from the 'churchy' image of stained-glass windows and old ladies in hats" (Combe, 1997). Much to the delight of the church, clothing designers, luxury car makers, and other corporate actors were eager to place their products in a church commercial.

Those in the marketing profession, in their more reflective moments, recognize the ambiguity of the Church of England's newfound enthusiasm for corporate-style selling. "Britain's churches aren't really full of BMW-driving blondes," said one editorial, "and anyone who turns up expecting that will be sorely disappointed by the patterned sweaters and sensible shoes of a genuine C of E congregation" (*Marketing,* 1997, p. 3). While one church ad director asserts that "unless people can be persuaded that Christianity really is unique and worthwhile [via ad campaigns] they will simply go to the cinema, play bingo or go down to the pub"(Combe, 1997), those elsewhere in the industry are more realistic:

If people want rock concerts, raves, youth activities or a place to chat, there are plenty of secular companies quite willing to supply these needs and better able to do so than any of our churches. The Nine o'Clock Service v. The Ministry of Sound [a pop group]? No contest. Oasis at Wembley v. Christian Rock at St. Jude's? A no-brainer.

A Christian church which attempts to compete with secular entertainments on its own terms [as promised in recent church ad campaigns] is doomed to failure (*Marketing,* 1997, p. 3).

The sensibilities attendant to using culture-industry tactics to promote Christianity are not self-limiting; in fact, they can and do influence other aspects of church life. Having decided that market research, focus groups, and audience-friendly pitches are the way to revive the Church of England, it seems only consistent that the Archbishop of Canterbury wants liturgies that cater more to prospective audiences—specifically, shorter services, punchier sermons, and more generally "less churchy, less clerical, less overtly religious." He claims that "I have a theory that more people would come to church if they know the service would not go on more than one hour" (*Daily Telegraph,* 1999). Another Anglican bishop has urged churches to rearrange liturgy times in order not to conflict with popular football matches (McIllroy and Combe, 1997).

For the Vatican, preparing for many papal Masses during Holy Year 2000, many debates arose regarding how to make the liturgies more television-friendly—specifically, how to make them shorter, livelier, and more likely to hold at-home viewers. Several European television producers asked the Vatican Television Center to make a number of changes in the papal liturgies— shorter liturgies, edited-for-broadcast Masses, innovations including "more remote-control cameras, a greater variety of camera positions, and even pre-recorded material. And why not invite guest directors from all over the world to try out some fresh TV ideas during jubilee events?" (Thavis, 1999). Monsignor Ugo Moretto, director of the Vatican Television Center, expressed sympathy for the problems of the broadcast networks, but wondered aloud "Are we making a spectacle or a liturgy? And are the two compatible?" At present, there are some outer limits beyond which liturgies will not be bent to satisfy the imperatives of television: as Moretto observed, "You can't tell the pope he has to keep his sermon under seven minutes" (Thavis, 1999).

There is nothing inevitable about the church's transformation into yet another culture industry. The Missionaries of Charity—Mother Theresa's religious community—has steadfastly refused all requests to use the founder's image and name in promotional campaigns, even for causes she supported; the community's numbers continue to grow (despite passing on such cross-promotional possibilities) while others continue to plummet. There are some depths to which even mainstream churches will not stoop: while Britain's Anglicans and Catholics supported an Easter ad blitz a few years ago that studiously avoided all cruciform imagery because such had tested as depressing to audiences, both ultimately quit a church advertising network that recently produced a millennium ad campaign that substituted Disney, Coca-Cola, Kodak, and other transnationals for the apostles in Da Vinci's "Last Supper" painting (the part of Judas was given to Microsoft) (Glendhill, 1999).

Nevertheless, the urge to rely on advertising, marketing, and public relations remains strong and on the rise. While the churches' own capacities for formation erode—in part a consequence of the cultural ecology of for-profit culture industries—the formative powers of the media conglomerates (some of which use and degrade Christian resources in the process) will continue to increase. The intriguing question is not whether capitalist culture will continue to shape hearts and imaginations more thoroughly than the Way of the Cross, but whether the churches will produce people able to tell the difference between the two.

4

The Church and the Death Business

Descriptions of the increased influence of for-profit corporations over church-related projects; the adoption of ruthless business practices that impact adversely on the poor; and the loss of Christian identity and mission in the interest of greater market share and profitability often appear in discussions about Christian higher education and whether church-affiliated colleges and universities differ in any substantive ways from their state counterparts. Such descriptions also find voice in debates about whether or not religiously affiliated hospitals and healthcare institutions have become interchangeable with the market-driven, cost-cutting behemoths that are transforming the health care "industry."

We could use these well-worked examples to illustrate the convergence and consolidation of Christianity Incorporated, but we won't. Instead, we will focus on an intersection of liturgical and business practice where corporate power has only recently begun flexing its muscle, where the accommodation of church thought and practice to capitalist norms is underway but as yet unfinished. We are talking about death and the death industry, especially with reference to developments affecting the Catholic Church.

The corporate transformation of funerals, burials, memorials, and other aspects of death and bereavement has advanced rapidly and largely beneath the radar of public awareness. By acquiring family-owned funeral homes and nonprofit cemeteries, by centralizing functions and driving competitors into bankruptcy, and by dominating local markets in order to raise prices by 30 percent and more, a handful of death-industry firms have captured 25 percent of the funeral market in the United States. Death conglomerates hope to bring the same degree of market concentration (and the profit margins typical of oligopoly) that once typified the auto and petrochemical industries into the mom-and-pop world of neighborhood funeral homes, local cemeteries, and headstone makers.

The corporate move to rationalize death—the business side of death, anyway—brings such firms squarely into a longstanding area of church ministry and practice. While funeral and burial processes in the United States for decades have been organized by family-owned businesses, care for the dead, remembrance of the departed, and support for the grieving have long been central to the pastoral life of the church. Among the corporal (or "bodily") works of mercy, burying the dead has been a consistent, albeit usually understated, component that joins the living and the dead in the praise and service of God. As a movement that denies death the last word in human existence, Christianity witnesses to the gospel by how it treats the dead as well as by how it treats the living. While church practices regarding death have exhibited substantial variation across cultures and eras, the importance of death, resurrection, and continuing on the Way has remained relatively constant.

Less apparent, however, is how large a financial stake the churches have in contemporary practices of caring for the dead. For many Catholic dioceses, revenues from their ownership of cemeteries has long been one of the single largest sources of Church income; unsold cemetery plots appear on Church ledgers as important sources of future revenue. Given that an acre of cemetery land can produce between $3–5 million in revenue (Harris, 1997, pp. 86–89), the Church's ministry to the dead and grieving has long struggled to balance matters liturgical and lucrative, caring for the dead and the bottom line at the same time.

For all their financial importance, Catholic cemeteries for decades existed as a rather sleepy, often overlooked aspect of Church organization and practice. They did relatively little advertising or marketing, their position relatively secure given that most Catholics opted for a funeral Mass and subsequent burial on Church-approved land. Catholics were told that only consecrated ground was appropriate for a Catholic's final resting place.

While most churchgoers might be only dimly aware of the Church's cemetery holdings, the bishops have long been aware of their importance. Indeed, state legislators across the country have many stories about the zeal with which the Church has exerted its political clout to defend its cemeteries from encroachments, unwanted regulations, or other threats to their financial health.

While the diocese owned the cemeteries and sometimes the above-ground mausoleums, other aspects of the system—funerals, monuments, cremations, and many other details—were mostly family-owned concerns that were known on occasion to reduce costs for indigent families, both out of compassion and to maintain a good reputation among pastors, clergy, and religious leaders in their communities. Even at its best, this decentralized system was rife with abuses and exploitation, and hardly a picture of other-regarding localism; the targets of Jessica Mitford's 1963 classic *The American Way of Death* were almost all small family-owned enterprises. Still, from the perspective of Church leaders, the overall management of death was fairly straightforward—Catholic cemeteries owned by the Church, an array of independent funeral and funeral-related providers that maintained good relations with the Church, and a steady stream of revenue that financed numerous Church ministries, charities, and operations.

It is this set of arrangements—from which the Church has profited for so long—that is under direct assault by the rapid transformations wrought by the transnational death industries. Like local retailing falling beneath the corporate wheels of Wal-Mart and similar firms, small funeral homes, cemeteries, and associated industries are being taken over or driven out by firms that aim for monopoly or near-monopoly power and profit margins far above previous industry averages. And the stakes are large: death purchases in the United States are more than $10 billion per year, and more than $40 billion may be tied up in prepaid death arrangements (see Krueger, 1998; also Werner, 1999, p. 7).

Church leaders find themselves in the middle of these industrial changes and upheavals, trying to achieve several potentially
incompatible objectives. The business practices of the corporate
giants threaten a primary source of diocesan revenues in many
ways; the giants' aggressive marketing tactics and jacked-up prices
fall hardest on the poorest members of their congregations; and
the firms' substitution of sentiment and ersatz compassion for
more substantive Christian practices of mercy and mutuality further erodes an important expression of discipleship and ecclesial
solidarity.

What makes the case of the death industry so interesting from
an ecclesiological perspective is precisely its undetermined outcome. The corporate takeover of death is well underway, but not
yet a fait accompli. To protect its revenue stream, many Church
leaders are imitating or joining the corporate giants, to the likely
detriment (as we will argue) of other Christian objectives and priorities—but even here, matters remain unsettled. The corrosion
of death as an occasion for the upbuilding of the body of Christ is
accelerated by the appropriation of hitherto Christian responsibilities by transnational firms, but other paths still remain visible.

While the final chapters remain to be written, the trends are
not promising. And the trendsetters, those calling the tune to
which the Church is expected to dance, are the leaders of the for-
profit revolution in death.

McDonald's Meets the Mortician

One of the company's nearly 29,000 workers will treat [SCI Chairman Robert Waltrip's] body just like the others they handle each
day: It will be sprayed with disinfectant, and his throat and anus
will be packed with gauze to prevent fluids from leaking. His mouth
will be closed with glue or sewn shut by a thread run through his
septum and lower gum. His eyes will be closed with plastic eye-
caps or glue. Then an incision will be made in his throat, upper
arm, or pelvis, and embalming fluid—a solution of methyl alcohol
or formaldehyde—will be pumped into his body, forcing all the
blood out. Waltrip, a large man of perhaps 250 pounds, will require

about five gallons of embalming fluid. Upon completion, another worker will dab a bit of makeup on his face and hands and ship him back to the SCI location handling the arrangements, where he'll be dressed in one of his many dark suits.

There's nothing romantic or sentimental about preparing a corpse for the grave, but that's the point: Waltrip . . . has made himself a very rich man by taking sentimentality out of the funeral trade and replacing it with a tough—some might say ruthless—business mentality (Bryce, 1996, p. 58).

Had Jessica Mitford not lived long enough to see it firsthand, the thought of family-owned funeral homes becoming the good guys in the industry would surely have had her spinning in her ash urn. Perhaps "good guys" is inappropriate, given that the dubious sales approaches, overpriced sentimentality, and grief-for-hire she described still typifies much of the industry. Maybe "less bad" is a more apt description, given the rise of an even more mercenary alternative: publicly traded, mammoth conglomerate chains that aim to dominate the business of death. Next to them, the family funeral directors don't look so shady.

At present three firms—Service Corporation International (SCI), Stewart Enterprises, and the Loewen Group—control roughly one-fourth of the funeral business in the United States and Canada (and are an important presence in many overseas markets as well). These firms have been the leaders in consolidating ownership of funeral homes, cemeteries, monument companies, crematories, and other parts of the death industry; given that such corporate takeovers are a relatively recent phenomenon, the speed of transformation is noteworthy. And while several of the giants are experiencing serious problems of their own at present, the process will almost surely continue at a rapid rate.

These three firms have all pursued broadly similar acquisition strategies. A chain will buy one or more funeral homes in a given area, keeping the establishment's name and often its staff and former owners as employees. The community reputation and image is an asset the firms seeks to preserve by obscuring or hiding its ownership position (no signs advertising, for example, "An SCI outlet—millions and millions served"). The firm typically cuts expenses by centralizing operations—a fleet of vehicles that serve a number of funeral homes rather than separate hearses for each, consolidating purchasing and billing—but costs to consumers typically go up, rather than down. The strategy is usually called "clustering"—expenses are lowered via combined operations, while prices rise due to decreased competition and the need to meet Wall Street profit expectations. Prices go up considerably, in fact—being buried by a McDeath provider costs at least 30 percent more compared to an independent undertaker, and in some markets it is substantially more than that.

The clustering strategy of the chains guarantees they will enjoy market power far beyond that suggested by mere ownership statistics. By concentrating their acquisitions in targeted areas, the chains establish monopoly or oligopoly positions for themselves—and since most people won't ship a departed loved one dozens or hundreds of miles away in search of a lower price, the chains are able to reap large profits. In fact, the arrival of death chains in a given community usually impels or allows independent homes to raise their own prices dramatically—in part to because they must now make more money off the funerals they do secure to compensate for business siphoned off by the chains, and in part simply because they can boost their prices significantly and still be cheaper than conglomerates. The upward racheting of prices has outpaced inflation for the past decade or so (in Florida, for example, the cost of dying rose three times faster than the cost of living during the 1990s; see Krueger, 1998), and has been especially burdensome for poor people.

Recently, the California Department of Consumer Affairs surveyed 169 cities regarding ownership of funeral homes. It found that conglomerates owned all of the funeral homes in 44 percent of these municipalities (Calpirg, 1998). In Washington state, chains now own 49 percent of funeral homes, according to the *Seattle Times;* funeral costs there rose by 65 percent from 1992 to 1996, according to one analyst, "because the real client is no longer the family of the deceased but the stockholder" (Newman, 1997). Another observer notes that SCI and Loewen now control at least 25 percent of the funeral trade in Florida, "considered the El

Dorado of the death business," because of its concentration of older residents (Larson, 1996).

A major investigation by the New York City Department of Consumer Affairs revealed a pattern of industry concentration that paid special attention to ethnic and religious segmentation in death practices. SCI, the dominant corporate actor in New York City, has established an especially powerful position in the Jewish funeral enclave: the firm owns fourteen of the city's twenty-eight Jewish funeral homes, including six of the seven Jewish establishments in Manhattan. Both in its Jewish and non-Jewish establishments, SCI prices are substantially higher than its few remaining competitors; but with so many establishments owned behind the scenes by the same company, comparison shopping can all too easily become a sham exercise involving properties of the same parent firm. According to Consumer Affairs commissioner Jules Polonetsky, "Currently the choice for some consumers is between one SCI-owned funeral home or another SCI-owned funeral home" (Department of Consumer Affairs, 1999).

The conglomerates have also focused on increasing their hitherto modest presence among African-American funeral enterprises. Long a mainstay of black communities, black-owned funeral homes look like especially attractive acquisitions since white Protestants have turned increasingly toward cremation rather than full-fledged burials (for instance, one industry estimate claims that 80 percent of whites in San Francisco choose cremation, while in 1998 cremations outnumbered burials in Florida for the first time). African-Americans, Asians, Latinos, and (to a somewhat lesser extent) Catholics are now prime conglomerate target audiences "precisely because these groups still hold to traditional funerals and have not participated in the great shift among white Protestants: toward cremation and bodiless memorials, away from store-bought funeral services with an expensively embalmed body on view in an expensive casket" (Larson, 1996). One of the conglomerates (Loewen) entered into a sweetheart deal with the Reverend Henry Lyons, then head of the National Baptist Convention, as a way to increase its market share in the black community. Black funeral directors cried sellout and favoritism; Lyons was later convicted on racketeering and fraud charges and sentenced to prison, but the chains remain intent on buying up black-owned funeral homes.

Even the economic disadvantages of minority communities (and the high mortality rate among African-American males) are attractive to the funeral industry. Economist Dwayne Banks describes how the "Nike mentality" prompts many poor inner-city families to spend lavishly on funerals:

> In this society we're valued by our material possessions—not only by what we have but by our ability to purchase things. So if you look at the cultural context of the inner cities, it makes sense: the way of showing you valued the deceased is by providing in death what you couldn't provide in life.

The paradox of expensive funerals assumed by poor families is explained in part, according to Banks, by community support. "You might not be able to get together the money for college, but death brings about this sense of communalism. For a funeral, a family will pull resources together and the church will contribute. It's what people dream of America being" (quoted in Newman, 1997).

In addition to cutting costs and raising prices, the corporate consolidators are bringing the full weight of advanced advertising and marketing techniques to the industry. All of the tools described in chapter 4—psychographic research, database manipulation, focus groups, test-marketing, and the like—are placed at the service of firms responsible for providing double-digit profits to investors (see for example Schafer, 1997).

Industry analysts know that despite the huge expense of an American-style funeral—for many people their largest single expenditure other than a house or car—most people are ignorant of the funeral planning process and (if buying when someone has just died) are emotionally ill-equipped to resist the gentle suggestions and assistance of experienced funeral directors (a Loewen document for investors describes this as among the "attractive industry fundamentals"; see Larson, 1996). "Customers typically conduct little, if any, comparative shopping and display a high degree of loyalty to firms to which they have been referred or which they have used previously. As a result, the industry tends to enjoy 'significant pricing flexibility'"—which means firms may increase prices liberally without losing much business, according to industry stock analyst Susan Little (see Davis, 1997, pp. 66–68).

A common sales tactic pioneered by Loewen is "Third Unit Target Merchandising." Years of market research and experience have convinced Loewen's sales planners that most consumers of caskets—usually the most expensive piece of a funeral package—will avoid the two cheapest models on display and buy the "third unit" from the bottom. After acquiring an independent funeral home, Loewen and other consolidators immediately raise casket prices, especially among the lower-end offerings, in order to boost sales revenue derived from the "third unit." To make inexpensive caskets as unattractive as possible, corporate homes usually keep economy models out of sight in rooms most consumers don't know exist; for consumers who insist on seeing caskets cheaper than those on offer in the main showrooms, they are often escorted to dingy facilities to view models offered deliberately in hideous colors and styles (like "grasshopper green" or ugly shades of purple) in order to push them toward more expensive options.

Advertising and marketing by the chains are especially aggressive in the area of pre-need sales. Corporate pressure to keep stock prices high by delivering big profits to investors translates into relentless pressures on salespeople to enroll future customers via pre-need contracts (only a few years ago, Loewen boasted of gross profits of 41.5 percent, while SCI enjoyed 25.3 percent profits from its funeral operations). An SCI manual for its pre-need salesforce dictates they must sell $1.50 of pre-need funerals for every $1 sold at need (when someone has just died) or risk losing their jobs. "In these situations, the arrangements environment is skewed toward meeting the salespersons' quota, not meeting the need of consumers," according to one consumer group (FAMSA FTC Comments, 1999). Some analysts suggest that grieving families are most vulnerable to hard sell pre-need appeals during the first two months following a loved one's death, precisely the time when salespeople descend to encourage future arrangements by the survivors. SCI now boasts of several billion dollars of pre-need funerals on its books, while consumer groups worry about uneven or inconsistent regulation of prepaid funds, fraud, and unexpected at-need charges.

The corporate takeover of death means more than acquiring funeral homes, of course. Despite some short-term setbacks (Loewen's cemetery acquisitions did not meet the firm's profit expectations, for example), vertical integration among the conglomerates is already well developed. The major firms now buy cemeteries, crematories, monument companies, florists, and more, creating the "all-in-one funeral-burial option" (Rotstein, 1999). As with funeral homes, this consolidation has tended to crush independent providers, raise costs, and inhibit competition. As with funeral homes, corporate ownership of these other industries is often hidden or obscured.

The chains have even managed to make money from what has long been the mortal enemy of the trade—cremation. The number of people cremated increased by 50 percent between 1987 and 1997, according to the Cremation Society of North America. One in four people nationally now choose cremation over burial (see Libbon, 1999), with substantial regional variations: half of all Nevadans choose cremation, as do 41 percent of Californians, compared with only 3 percent of Alabama residents (see Horn, 1998).

In the face of such trends, the corporate death firms have taken the lead in exploring the profit potentials of cremation. The object is to push cremation prices (a basic immediate cremation can cost as little as a few hundred dollars) up ever closer to the price of a body burial (a typical funeral, plot, and burial averages around $10,000, according to some industry figures). One way to do so is to require family members to do an "identification viewing" before cremation—to make sure, in other words, that the right body is going to the crematory. The need for such a viewing is not obvious, assuming a minimally competent funeral director who doesn't need customers checking on the accuracy of any other part of his or her work. However, such an identification viewing has become a common means to induce families to purchase an expensive cremation container for the dead. For those who initially refuse to do so, suggests one consultant, "make sure you show them Mom's body in the cardboard box. Someone in the family is bound to say, 'Maybe we should get something nicer.'" This one step, according to the consultant, can "add $1400 to each cremation call" (Horn, 1998).

Other profit potential resides in the market for cremation urns (a single deceased can prompt the purchase of multiple urns, if survivors can be persuaded that each should have a portion of the "cremains" for themselves). Just as the industry has developed a market for expensive cremation body containers—which will be burned along with the deceased—so has it boosted the purchase of high priced urns by presenting unsold family members with ashes in a cardboard box stamped "Temporary" in bold letters. Lockets (to hold a small amount of ashes), memorials, scattering services, interment or burial of cremated remains—all can add to the expense of a simple cremation, making for robust corporate profits in what was once seen as a threat to the industry; indeed, given the minimal costs of a cremation, their profit margins are higher than those for a traditional funeral. Given all this, it is no surprise that Stewart added the largest cremation group in the country, Sentinel Cremation Services, to its corporate holdings in 1997.

The Consolidation of the Consolidators

Not everything among the McDeath giants goes well, however. The race to expand as rapidly as possible while continuing to pay high dividends to investors has led to a major financial collision among the three largest firms. One of them is dead, or at least bankrupt; another is seriously ill, but will probably recover; and the third took a short-term beating but will probably profit considerably from the misfortunes of the other two.

The biggest loser thus far is the Loewen Group, once the darling of Wall Street boosters who were impressed by the company's mid-1990s profit margins of over 40 percent (a level that proved its unsustainability as founder Ray Loewen accelerated acquisitions in an effort to keep profits high via short-term consolidation advantages). Driven to outperform the larger, more powerful SCI, Loewen often overpaid for funeral homes, saw disappointing returns from its rapid move into cemetery ownership, and reeled from a Mississippi jury's $500 million judgment against it for illegal and predatory practices against a family-owned funeral home. The Canadian-owned Loewen has appealed the award as a violation of NAFTA on the grounds that Mississippi's civil justice system falls short of international standards of fairness, and also that the award constituted expropriation without compensation—another violation of NAFTA's many corporate protections (Kingsnorth, 1999, pp. 11–12). The firm eventually settled for $150 million.

As if overexpansion and poor management were not enough, Loewen also suffered due to the good health of North Americans—milder than usual winters and other factors made for lower than expected death rates in the mid-to-late 1990s. Longer life spans for thousands of people translated into a death sentence for Loewen.

Having rejected a buyout offer from SCI at $45-to-$50 per share as recently as 1996, Loewen saw its stock plummet below the $1 per share minimum required for listing on the New York Stock Exchange in 1999; its debt rating had been downgraded to junk-bond status by 1998 (see Verberg, 1998, pp. 71–72). The firm filed for Chapter 11 bankruptcy on June 1, 1999, and it now operates under a restructuring plan that includes a substantial selloff of many its properties at drastically reduced prices.

Loewen may be dead for now (but since large corporations seldom seem to stay dead these days, it will likely rise again), but SCI isn't faring too well either. Still the dominant player among the corporate death firms, SCI has seen its own earnings and stock price tumble from its mid-90s levels. If Wall Street boosters were surprised by Loewen's fall from grace, fewer still were prepared for SCI's financial woes: stock analyst Susan Little remained bullish on the firm throughout the 1990s, even predicting a stock price at $60 by early 1997 (Bryce, 1996, p. 58). Neither she nor her compatriots among industry watchers saw what was coming—a drop in earnings and a stock collapse (losing more than 40 percent of its value in one day)—down to $4 per share in early 2000 (from $35 in 1999 and $45 in 1998; see, among others, Bryce, 1999).

Some of SCI's problems may reflect growing pains incurred following the decision to buy the nation's fourth-largest death chain, Equity Corporation, in the late 1990s. Investor concerns about SCI's management of prepaid funds, fears of greater regulatory scrutiny, and high levels of executive compensation contributed to the firm's current troubles.

Despite these recent problems, however, SCI remains far and away the most powerful force in the industry. It owns more than 3,800 funeral homes, 520 cemeteries, and 198 crematoria; it also operates in twenty foreign countries on five continents (Bryce, 1999). SCI performs 14 percent of all funerals in the United Kingdom, 25 percent in Australia, and 28 percent in France (it now does more than half a billion dollars in business in France annually). While it rebounds in its domestic operations, SCI looks to expand its presence overseas, given the lax regulatory environment it encounters in many countries (although having politically well-connected board members like former U.S. representative and cabinet official Tony Coelho greasing the skids into Portugal, Spain, and Argentina also helps considerably).

With Loewen dead (or dying) and SCI wounded, the big winner in the consolidation process thus far is Stewart Enterprises. While still dwarfed by SCI (Stewart owns nearly 800 funeral homes, compared to SCI's 3,800), Stewart is positioned to benefit most from the hardships of its rivals. As noted by Daniel Fisher in *Forbes*:

> First, the world's biggest funeral chains exhausted themselves with an abortive takeover battle [SCI's unwanted offer to Loewen]. Then they went on a buying binge . . . [Stewart's] two biggest competitors essentially knocked themselves out, leaving Stewart with an open field in which to expand—just as millions of baby boomers approach the age when their next big purchase could be a cemetery plot instead of a new BMW (1999, p. 77).

Fisher and other observers attribute Stewart's good health to its unwillingness to overpay for properties—SCI and Loewen often bid up prices for local firms they both sought—and to sticking with funeral homes rather than branching out quickly into ceme-

teries and ancillary industries. While its competitors hemorrhaged
money in 1998, Stewart showed a nearly 22 percent growth in
annual sales (Strout, 1999, p. 18). While Stewart's stock prices
have declined more than 30 percent in recent months—as
investors fled all big death firms in the wake of the SCI-Loewen
downturn—its stock still trades well above that of its competitors.

More significantly, Stewart stands to benefit from the distress
of its rivals as it buys funeral homes at cut-rate prices. SCI has cut
its acquisitions budget by two-thirds, Loewen is selling hundreds
of properties, and Stewart is boosting its acquisitions spending
(although in absolute terms SCI is still the biggest spender on consolidation). Stewart is poised to buy big in a market where sell-
ers have fewer options than they did two years ago.

While some investors remain skeptical of the death firms' ability to continue delivering big profits, there seems to be no turning back from a funeral market increasingly dominated by a few
firms. Despite its recent problems, according to Josh Rosen of
Credit Suisse First Boston, "fundamentally the death services
industry is an attractive industry" (quoted in Bryce, 1999). The
much-anticipated boom in Baby Boomer deaths will still arrive,
and if they can finesse the challenges posed by cremation, the
death firms will thrive in the years ahead even as their small independent competitors wither away. In the midst of all this sits the
Catholic Church and its huge cemetery interests—uncertain, hes-
itant, and tempted by the prospect of an extraordinary financial
windfall.

The Church and the Death Industry

Church leaders surveying the dramatically changed economic
and cultural landscape usually identify two alternative directions—to embrace the new order represented by the death conglomerates, or to protect as much of the status quo as possible by
keeping the chains at arms length while adopting many of their
tactics. A third option—to resist the chains *and* move beyond the
status quo by reclaiming death and burial practices for the church—

exists, although it does not appear on the radar screens of most church leaders.

Option One: Joining the Giants

Setting the terms of discussion across the board is the 1997 partnership between the Archdiocese of Los Angeles—largest in the United States—and Stewart Enterprises, one of the Big Three death conglomerates. This deal allows Stewart to construct and run nine for-profit mortuaries on the grounds of Archdiocesan cemeteries, an arrangement that has left other conglomerates scrambling to secure diocesan partners of their own while church officials elsewhere watch with a mix of fear and excitement.

While the general terms of the Los Angeles deal are known, the particulars remain secrets held closely by the principals. The Archdiocese receives an undisclosed rent from Stewart, while the company pockets all proceeds from funeral arrangements. Most of the mortuaries will include chapels, and all will offer one-stop shopping for flowers, monuments, and other funeral and burial components.

According to the *Los Angeles Times,* Stewart's other funeral holdings in Los Angeles and Orange counties are substantially more expensive than their independent competitors—a price difference ranging from 10 to 70 percent. Stewart hopes to capture a substantial share of funerals for persons buried in Archdiocesan cemeteries; the first four Catholic cemeteries receiving Stewart mortuaries perform more than ten thousand burials annually (Fields, 1999), making them a lucrative fishing hole for Stewart's initial efforts.

For its part, Archdiocesan officials look at the Stewart partnership as a way to increase the number of burials in Catholic cemeteries; according to Church consultants, the proportion of Catholics buried in Archdiocesan cemeteries declined from 85 percent in 1965 to 35 percent in 1985 (Wirpsa, 1998a). Given the importance of Catholic cemeteries as "the number-one money-generating department in the diocese," according to an Archdiocesan spokesman, chancery officials saw the Stewart partnership as a way to win back customers with the offer of all-in-one death arrangements—which Stewart's chief executive Joseph Henican optimistically projects to add between 2,000 and 4,000 new burials annually for the Church in the first six cemetery-mortuary sites (Fields, 1999).

Stewart has lost no time exploiting its intimate relationship with the Archdiocese. It runs ads in the Church's English- and Spanish-language newspapers, and has begun aggressive pre-need sales campaigns using lists obtained from the Archdiocese. Anecdotal evidence of customers who interpret the arrangement as Catholic "endorsement" of Stewart's facilities, program, and prices is already accumulating (see for example Field, 1999). In fact, James Tixier, the director of the Archdiocese's pre-need cemetery sales, acknowledged that Church cemetery personnel will consider Stewart "a natural referral," although doing so does not—in his eyes—constitute a recommendation of Stewart over other funeral homes. Stewart's policy of naming its mortuaries after the Catholic cemeteries in which they reside furthers the impression of ecclesial recommendation of Stewart over other providers (Wirpsa, 1998a).

In addition to providing Stewart with church mailing lists, the Archdiocese has extended the firm other advantages that put its smaller, family-owned competitors at a disadvantage. Foremost among these in the long term may be the decision to allow funeral Masses to be performed in Stewart's on-site chapels—a privilege denied other funeral homes because, unlike them, Stewart's homes sit on "consecrated ground," namely, the Catholic cemetery land. Stewart's sales representatives can then use this privilege as a selling point, a way to avoid church-to-cemetery transport charges other homes levy since for them a funeral Mass requires use of a church off cemetery grounds. This "savings" is overmatched, however, by the higher fees Stewart homes charge for most other parts of the package.

The Stewart–Los Angeles deal has had a major impact on church-and-death dealings across the country. One industry analyst noted that "the entire industry is watching" the unfolding. "If this takes off, I see them all taking a look at it" (Fields, 1999). In fact, Stewart's competitors have wasted no time in the aftermath of the Los Angeles venture in pursuing their own church-based strategies.

Stewart's biggest competitor, SCI, responded to the Los Angeles move by creating Christian Funeral Services, Inc., a wholly owned subsidiary "dedicated to the management of funeral homes, cemeteries and related assets for Catholic dioceses throughout North America" (SCI Press Release, 1997). CFS is chaired by Matthew J. Lamb, a prominent Chicago Catholic businessman whose chain of twelve funeral homes was bought by SCI in 1987.

One of Lamb's first moves to increase the visibility of CFS was to donate $175,000 to the North American College in Rome, where American seminarians go for study and where American bishops frequently reside when in town for Vatican meetings. Playing up Lamb's Chicago connections, the gift will pay for a suite in honor of the late Cardinal Joseph Bernadin of Chicago and a chapel honoring the current Chicago leader, Francis George. CFS already owns one of the largest funeral homes in North America on the grounds of the Basilica of Notre Dame in Montreal. It also manages cemetery properties for other parts of the Church, including the Diocese of Dallas.

The Loewen Group, the third of the major death firms, followed Stewart's Los Angeles coup by signing a long-term deal to manage cemeteries for the Diocese of Tucson. Stewart itself, while boasting of its Los Angeles deal in its annual report, describes it as the first step among many as it plans to deepen its existing relationships with seventy dioceses in thirty-nine states (1999 annual report). The Los Angeles model also operates in New Orleans, where Stewart owns a mausoleum on church grounds and manages sales of mausoleum space for the archdiocese.

Option Two: Corporate Tactics Without the Corporation

While some dioceses have already thrown in with the for-profit conglomerates, the majority of Catholic cemetery leaders are wary of the power of the corporations. Nevertheless, they recognize the many social changes affecting Catholic death practices—increases in cremation rates, large numbers of Catholics being courted by for-profit cemeteries, and pressures from bishops for cemeteries to generate more money for other diocesan programs.

Thus far, as reflected by organizations like the National Catholic Cemetery Association, most dioceses are working to maintain the status quo of Church burials, a funeral Mass, and a strong, steady revenue stream into chancery coffers. While they hope to do this without becoming tied to the conglomerates, increasingly many Church institutions have adopted the same tactics used by the for-profit powerhouses.

The Diocese of Pittsburgh, for example, has adopted an aggressive posture in defending its powerful regional position (86 percent of the faithful still choose one of the fifteen Catholic cemeteries in the diocese). The diocese created the Catholic Funeral Plan, in which "families purchase insurance that locks in the current price of funeral costs with a participating funeral home, and in doing so they're reminded of the Church's emphasis on a final Mass and other Catholic rituals" (Rotstein, 1999). The plan is in addition to the diocese's movement into selling burial monuments and other hitherto separate parts of the funeral and burial package.

Local funeral directors claim the Catholic Funeral Plan amounts to unfair competition given the diocese's marketing of the plan directly in parishes. James Hahn, President of the Pennsylvania Funeral Directors Association, notes that "We can all compete against free enterprise—you can't compete against God." The diocese is being sued by the Monument Dealers of Pennsylvania for antitrust violations, and by the Pittsburgh school district for using its tax-exempt status to protect its profits from monument sales (Rotstein, 1999).

Elsewhere, the Diocese of Cleveland, which stopped selling coffin vaults and headstones in 1996, resumed their sale in 1998 to offset cemetery losses. The same charges of unfair competition and illegal use of tax-exempt status greeted the change (Newsnet 5, 1998). In Detroit, the archdiocese became the first to construct a crematorium on Catholic cemetery property, a direct response to competitive pressures from conglomerates (Schall, 2000).

While the particulars vary across dioceses, defending the status quo has involved substantially more aggressive pre-need sales, beefed-up marketing through Church and secular channels, and moves toward one-stop shopping through Catholic cemetery organizations or spinoffs. Some of these efforts may include selective partnerships with the death conglomerates, an option that remains "on the minds of the vicars general, the moderators of the curia, [and] the diocesan cemetery directors" across the country, according to a consultant working with twenty dioceses in the United States and Canada (Wirpsa, 1998b). As Church leaders respond to the financial pressures brought by the chains, imitation of the latter's tactics—even some of the more dubious of them—seems to be an essential ingredient.

Option Three: Church-Centered Death Practices

Without question, this is the least developed—theologically, institutionally, and in terms of current ecclesial practices—of the three options. It also has the deepest roots in the Christian tradition, and is the best chance for the Church to resist the transformation of its ministry at the end of life into another commodified facet of Christianity Incorporated.

Before publicly traded conglomerates took over the industry, before the mortuary profession evolved from being a sideline of cabinet-makers and carpenters who made caskets during their slow months—before all of them, the church and families took care of the dead themselves in a variety of local and culturally distinctive ways. Not only did modernity's fear of death remove dying, death, and the body from the routines of families and neighbors, it also shoved aside the rituals, practices, and ministries of the church. Clergy became sidekicks to funeral directors, the lush interiors of funeral chapels displaced church settings, and church practices around and after death became disaggregated, decontextualized, and oftentimes stripped of their coherence.

As noted by one Canadian mortician (quoted in Wasielewski personal archive, n.d.):

By and large, the funeral industry has shaped the funeral ritual, and the customs associated with it, to its own benefit.

Most religious groups have stepped back and allowed the funeral director to define the social customs of the burial rite. As well, the funeral industry has learned to use religious customs against the consumer for financial exploitation.

Death became removed from its place in the primary Christian narratives of life, death, and resurrection, and was made over into grief management and therapeutic interventions for the living (making death even more tragic, and definitely more final, than in it is in the larger Christian tradition).

This third option involves reconstituting many old practices as part of new narratives and more deliberately ecclesiocentric patterns of Christian life. Different dioceses, congregations, and communities will combine elements in varying patterns, but they will share strong family resemblances built upon a rejection of expensive manufactured American burial practices, and upon a return of most elements of death and burial to the church community.

Some churches already do some or most of the primary tasks in a way that sustains the strong sense of continuity between the living and dead members of the body of Christ, even while it tightens the bonds between those living church members who minister to the dead and their families. The Archdiocese of Denver took a partial step toward church reclamation of death in 1980 by opening its own mortuary as a way to prevent price-gouging of the poor and elderly; according to a prominent Catholic critic of the funeral industry, the Denver facility "found that it could provide funerals for one-half the price of the lowest-price mortuary, while paying the highest wages in the area, building rent, and all taxes, fees and expenses of other mortuaries" (Wasielewski, n.d). While efforts like these aim to remedy the worst of consumer exploitation, most aspects of death and burial remain largely unchanged.

Somewhat more ambitiously, beginning in the mid-1980s several Catholic dioceses, parishes, and Knights of Columbus chapters in Canada began establishing co-operative mortuaries—incurring the wrath of for-profit providers and chains, one of whom asserted that "funerals don't belong in the church." By 1997, a dozen church co-op mortuaries in Canada were providing low-cost services by handling embalming, wakes, and services inside church buildings, and using large numbers of parishioners in this manifestation of the corporal and spiritual work of mercy.

Sometimes Christian care for the dead can build ecclesial or para-ecclesial bonds where none existed before. Such has been the experience of Debi Farris, a southern California housewife who took it upon herself to provide church burials and memorial services for dozens of infants abandoned at birth. What began as an effort to provide a Christian burial for a baby left in a gas station trash can evolved into a ministry that involves several dozen volunteers—senior citizens and high school students, police and medical personnel, and others. Her simple insistence that babies abandoned in life not also be abandoned in death has modeled several practices that congregations could usefully incorporate— including efforts to enable mothers to leave unwanted live infants at emergency facilities without fear of prosecution (Shindehette, 2000).

Other lessons emerge from the experiences of the Los Angeles Catholic Worker community, where hospice and in-house death care joined its existing work several years ago (Dietrich, 1996, p. 20). To members of this community, discipleship entails a different view of death and Christian responsibility than that on offer by commercialized dispositions.

Worker Jeff Dietrich follows social theorist Ivan Illich in asserting that

> because our homes have become inhospitable to death, they are also inhospitable to life. Much of the problem of advanced society stems from its enormous scale, which tends to overwhelm and dissipate community, initiative and spontaneous human response. What was once done in the home—the production of food, clothing, entertainment, education, the experience of birth and death— is all either provided or mediated by anonymous professionals. Those anonymous forces represent a form of death as they proceed to create a homogenized, dessicated, lifeless environment.

Dietrich recognizes that caring for the dying and the dead is hard work.

I, for one, prefer sitting in my room writing about it than actually sitting with the dying, or changing their diapers, or making their beds, or washing their bodies. It's all so personal, intimate, messy, human. And it takes a lot of work—a lot more than we thought it would.

But it is not just the physical labor that consumes us. It is the very palpable presence of death itself in our midst, sucking our energy like a vortex.

Dietrich and the Catholic Workers in Los Angeles do allow an undertaker to embalm the dead, but only after the community gathers around for its deathbed liturgy of prayers, Scripture reading, and a form of the rosary that combines the ancient meditation with recollections of the life of the deceased. After the undertaker performs his or her work, the body is returned to the Worker house for the community's usual Wednesday evening liturgy. Dietrich notes that

> newcomers can find it a little shocking to come to the Catholic Worker for Mass only to encounter a dead body in our living room. Some folks pass on dinner in the presence of the dead. We have had a number of our cremated friends buried here at the house or down at the [soup] kitchen so that they will always be with us.

For this third option to become viable—for the church to reclaim death as part of its bold story of mission and resurrection—more is needed than a few extra programs grafted onto the status quo. It requires, among other things, a positive conception of Christian death practices rooted more deeply in evangelization, catechesis, and mission than in therapeutic grief management for those still alive.

One of the best contemporary reflections on death, discipleship, and the church comes from theologian Thomas G. Long (1999). He notes that while Mitford performed a great service in exposing the profiteering sentimentality of the funeral industry, her own hostility to the body and ritual of almost any type prevented her from being very helpful to the church in its search for a more authentic incorporation of death.

Obviously, a genuine Christian funeral is not about the evils that Mitford found so easy to satirize—the vulgar, conspicuous consumption, the mawkish sentiment—but, strangely, a Christian funeral is also not primarily about many of the good things that its friends claim for it: the facilitation of grief, helping people to hold on to memories of the deceased, or even to supply pastoral care and comfort to the bereaved. A Christian funeral often provides these things, of course, but none of these is its central purpose. *A Christian funeral is nothing less than a bold and dramatic worship of the living God done attentive to and in the face of an apparent victory at the hands of the last enemy. Though the liturgy may be gently worded, there is no hiding the fact that, in a funeral, Christians raise a fist at death; recount the story of the Christ who suffered death, battled death, and triumphed over it; offer laments and thanksgiving to the God who raised Jesus from the grave; sing hymns of defiance; and honor the body and life of the saint who has died* (italics added).

Rather than being primarily a place to tell stories about the deceased, Long notes that

> the most important measure of a Christian funeral is its capacity to place the event of a person's death into the larger context of the Christian gospel. . . . The Christian funeral is a liturgical drama, a piece of gospel theater, with roles to play and a time honored, if flexible and culturally varied, script. . . . (T)hey are community enactments of a formative narrative.

It is in its liturgical tradition that the church still retains contact with preconsumerist death practices, and it is in liturgy that a path toward a more deeply renewed practice of church—involving life as well as death—may be found. As Long notes, Christian funeral rituals historically enacted stories of the deceased and his or her grand journey

> not to the land of the dead but into the presence of the living God, not over the River Styx but across the Jordan into the land of promise, flowing with milk and honey. For Christians, the deceased was not a ghoul to be feared nor an evil spirit to be warded off, but a saint to be respected, honored, loved, and accompanied with psalms, hymns, and prayers the last steps of the way (in the earli-

est Christian funerals, even given the kiss of peace). The dead body was neither a mere shell to be discarded as rubbish nor the totality of the person to be clutched and preserved in desperation, but a tangible sign, like the eucharistic bread, of God's gift of life.

To speak of liturgical renewal and a more central role for the church in dealing with the dead is not to ignore the tragic aspects of death.

By contrast [with sentimental commercial practices], the Christian funeral, at its best, speaks plainly of death. It does not shy away from naming death's power to pierce the human heart, to steal gifts of love, and to create empty places at the table of fellowship, and the Christian funeral bravely claims the victory over death won by Jesus Christ, and dares to trust the promise of the gospel's great mystery. "We shall not all die, but we will all be changed."

From Dying Individuals to a Living Church

To expect churches—Catholic and Protestant—to resist the commercialized horizons of for-profit conglomerates requires them to embody a stronger sense of church as primary community. A minimalist ecclesiology that makes few demands on its members, that dilutes the gospel to accommodate political and economic powers, is utterly incapable of resisting the trends that look to drag the churches into rising levels of death profiteering. In fact, the sort of civil religion typical of mainstream Christianity not only cannot resist such trends, it mostly fails to discern any but minor conflicts between such profiteering and the practices of discipleship.

As suggested previously, how the churches treat the dead is inseparable from how they treat the living. If a church is an association of individuals who share a fondness for an occasional worship hour and little more, then leaving them alone to cope with the sales tactics and fashions of the death firms seems unexceptional. If a church of individuals tries to preserve the status quo on death matters without strengthening its own sense of being a distinctive community and culture, it will almost surely continue to imitate and partner with the conglomerates until the few remaining differences between church practice and corporate practice will fade into an indistinguishable blur.

The church needs to stake out its own ground on matters of death, discipleship, and community—somewhere that is neither throwaway nor gaudy, neither abandonment nor spectacle. Perhaps the most appropriate liturgical parallel is with the Christian sacrament of marriage. Weddings are like funerals, in other words, at least when both are understood in relation to the witness of the body of Christ and the intended commercialization of those practices by for-profit firms.

For example, just as Christian marriage should be more than a crude contractual arrangement—legal, quick, and anonymous—so should Christian commemoration of the dead be more than an impersonal disposal that goes unnoticed by the community. Neither weddings nor death, however, should become exercises in conspicuous consumption, ostentatious indulgences of fashion, presentation, and status.

Similarly, the peer and societal pressures that dictate what constitutes a "proper" wedding or funeral can work to the detriment of the church as community (and especially of the poor, within and outside the church), and force the church to cater to the imperatives of market-driven and consumerist expectations. When the churches allow themselves to be used merely as markers of cultural transition—birth, marriage, death—they become incapable of developing any ecclesial understandings or practices that might go against the arbiters of fashion—be they for $30,000 wedding gowns or $30,000 caskets.

Although some church leaders have spoken out against exorbitant wedding expenditures and a handful have challenged exploitative funeral practices, most remain silent. They are unwilling to challenge the cultural norms that dominate their flock's ideas of what is reasonable, to what they are entitled, and what their "right" is to whatever sort of rite they desire. Most clergy resign themselves to playing an ancillary, supportive role—adding a liturgical gloss to a schedule in which the real action is not directed by the church. In such a context, the church doesn't rock the boat of market-defined expectations, although occasionally a church leader will intercede in individual cases in which hardship threatens a person's ability to enjoy comparable levels of social display. In weddings and funerals, in other words, the church's chaplaincy role dominates and inhibits all other ecclesial possibilities.

Without a revived liturgical imagination around matters of death—a revival that presupposes a concomitant ecclesial regeneration—the corporate takeover of death will likely proceed apace. Between the expensive death rituals of the conglomerates and the increasingly popular recourse to "anonymous" burials of Christians in Germany and elsewhere (see Downey, 1998; also *Christian Century,* 1996), the church must find its own unavoidably countercultural way to assert the gospel paradox that although we die, yet we live. Such a paradox the conglomerates cannot serve—they can only bury it.

5

John Locke in Ecclesial Drag?
The Problem with *Centesimus Annus*

Luke 18:18–25, rewritten according to the precepts contained in *Centesimus Annus*:

An official asked Jesus this question, "Good teacher, what must I do to inherit eternal life?" Jesus answered him, "Why do you call me good? No one is good but God. You know natural law and the commandments that follow from right reason." And he replied, "All of these I have observed from my youth." When Jesus heard this he said to him, "There is still one thing left for you: take all you have and invest it morally in order to aid the economic development of the poor, being sure that you receive sufficient profit to maintain your needs in a moderated lifestyle. Then come follow me." But when he heard this he became quite sad at the amount he would have to pay in transaction fees to his broker.

Jesus looked at the [now sad] official and said, "How hard it is for those who have no load mutual funds to enter the kingdom of God! For it is harder for a thread to pass through the eye of a needle than for a corporate executive with stock options to enter the kingdom of God."

Introduction

In 1991 Pope John Paul II promulgated the encyclical *Centesimus Annus* in order to commemorate the hundredth anniversary of Pope Leo XIII's *Rerum Novarum**. But *Centesimus* is quite a bit more than celebratory in character. In it, John Paul not only summarizes the Catholic Church's social teaching regarding politics and economics over the past century, but also advances and develops it more fully. Wittingly or not, what John Paul advances and develops is a vision of the church reacting to the world's impact on it rather than outlining the church's proactive impact on the world. Through his acceptance of liberal politics and economics, he lays and justifies the foundation for the church's cooperation with the corporate "spirituality and work" programs we have discussed in previous chapters and underwrites the efforts of the Woodstock Business Conference and other prominent Catholic apologists for capitalism such as George Weigel, Richard John Neuhaus, and Michael Novak.

In a significant passage John Paul writes:

> The church has no [economic] models to present; models that are real and truly effective can only arise within the framework of different historical situations through the efforts of all those who responsibly confront concrete problems in all their social, economic, political and cultural aspects as these interact with one another. For such a task the church offers her social teaching as an indispensable aid and ideal orientation, a teaching which, as already mentioned, recognizes the positive value of the market and of enterprise, but which at the same time points out that those need to be oriented toward the common good (43).

Stanley Hauerwas views this passage favorably, stating, "What is at stake is not an alternative 'model' of economics the church has put forward, but rather how the church stands as an alternative to *all* such models" (Hauerwas 1995, p.127). Yet if that charitable construction was John Paul's intent, the encyclical as a whole is a failure.

---

* Published in 1891, *Rerum Novarum* initiated the Roman Catholic Church's contemporary social doctrine and has been the wellspring for subsequent teachings on society. *Rerum* itself focused primarily upon the condition of workers and the relation between capital and labor.

What the pope describes and justifies in this passage and indeed throughout *Centesimus* is a chaplaincy church. In John Paul's view, the function of the church's social teaching is twofold: first, not to responsibly confront concrete problems in all their aspects (presumably because there are other social institutions more expert), but to provide an ideal orientation for these practical practitioners; and second, to try to moderate what he believes are "excessive" outcomes of corrupt institutions and practices. Thus John Paul simultaneously accepts and justifies those institutions and practices—at least in an abstract general sense—as normative, as the way economics, for example, ought to be, and then complains because the results of economics-as-it-ought-to-be are anti-Christian, unjust, and oppressive. The church does not offer a substantive alternative vision of the world in all its aspects (including economics) rooted in the gospel and faithful to Jesus' message, nor does it see itself as an alternative polity. Rather, the church described by John Paul sees itself as subordinated to the social reality of democratic politics and market economics. By accepting that subordination willingly and deferring to the power of the empires, the church relegates itself to the role of loyal cheerleader, commentator, and confessor.

This interpretation is borne out very early in the encyclical. John Paul states that the publication of *Rerum Novarum* in 1891 "created a lasting paradigm for the church," one which gives the church "citizenship status" amid the changing realities of public life (5). This position of citizenship provides the overall context for the church's function in the world:

> The church, in fact, has something to say about specific human situations, both individual and communal, national and international. She formulates genuine doctrine for those situations, a corpus which enables her to analyze social relations, to make judgments about them and to indicate directions to be taken for the just resolution of the problems involved (5).

We can leave aside for the moment the appearance that this passage seems to give license to the church to formulate economic and social models despite John Paul's earlier protestation to the contrary, and instead examine recent history. In fact, throughout the twentieth century in general and evident specifically in the social teaching of John Paul's pontificate, the Roman Catholic Church has had a great deal to say of a critical nature about the two rival social/cultural systems of this century—Marxism and democratic capitalism. Indeed, this trend of constructively criticizing the flaws and destructiveness of the social reality continues in many passages in *Centesimus* as John Paul examines triumphant democratic capitalism and its effects on workers, families, and communities. But John Paul misleads and confuses the church by the nature of this criticism and the overall context in which it occurs.

We certainly do not wish to imply that the pope or the church has nothing to say about specific human situations on any level, nor do we deny that the church ought to analyze and make judgments about the social realities abounding in the world. Quite the contrary. But we think also that it makes a great deal of difference where the church situates itself in offering criticism and direction to the world.

By accepting citizenship status, the church's fundamental attitude is loyalty and an alignment of itself and its goals with the world and its institutions. Rather, we should be proclaiming and arguing that the world's immediate and ultimate goals should be the same as the church's, and that the alignment should be reversed. It is certainly the case that Christians view themselves as members of the kingdom rather than citizens of the world.

This is more than a semantic difference. The inversion of the latter viewpoint entails that the church accept certain worldviews and the processes that flow from them as normative, which in the case of *Centesimus* mean the church's ultimate acceptance of liberal ideology. John Paul clearly affirms and argues in favor of the two main tenets of this ideology:

- that market capitalism is "the most efficient instrument for utilizing resources and effectively responding to needs" (34),
- and that the democratic state, characterized by respect for freedom and the defense of private property, is the ultimate

guarantor of human rights, dignity, and the just distribution of the wealth generated by the economic system (48).

This is, we believe, the main thrust of *Centesimus Annus*. But the issue before us and the church regarding this encyclical is not quite so simple.

The view we have just encapsulated is one of a Constantinian church subordinated to the economic and political order. While we reject that view, it is not in itself confusing or incoherent. But the vision of the church presented in the entirety of *Centesimus* is both.

For all the praise and support of market capitalism and democratic politics apparent in *Centesimus,* John Paul also spends a great deal of time outlining some of the disastrous effects and tendencies of those two aspects of liberal ideology. Yet John Paul does not seem to be aware that the disastrous effects he condemns are integral to the operation of a liberal culture; he speaks as though this "good" and "natural" theoretical system can be made to operate morally if not Christianly if only its "excesses" can be moderated. But those "excesses" he rightly decries are directly entailed by the theoretic model he embraces. By positing these two aspects of liberalism as justified in *Centesimus,* John Paul displays an incoherent approach to contemporary society, an approach that misleads and confuses the church. It is not surprising, then, that apologists for a liberal social order such as Neuhaus, Novak, and Weigel can find support for their position within *Centesimus* while at the same time antiliberal theorists such as David Schindler and (to a lesser extent) Stanley Hauerwas can point to *Centesimus* as inspiration and support for their contrary views. Both sides of this debate are correct: *Centesimus Annus* is so confused that each side of the controversy can find significant support for its analysis. Herein lies the most basic problem and failure of the encyclical.

In what follows we examine the major aspects of the theoretical foundation of economics and politics in *Centesimus* and show precisely how the inconsistency of John Paul's position arises and how the acceptance of liberal theory cannot yield the results John Paul desires or the gospel demands.

Building Toward the Theory of Church as Citizen: The Liberal Basis of *Centesimus Annus*

John Paul's logical starting point in the development of his economic and political theory as expressed in *Centesimus* is that of all liberal theorists from Hobbes and Locke to Rawls: the individual person. He uses the same concepts and language, and even structures his argument in the finest tradition of liberalism; in significant sections, John Paul's argument is indistinguishable from that of Locke in *The Second Treatise of Government*. In fact, John Paul's analysis of the individual and the individual's inherent characteristics (which is based in large measure on *Rerum Novarum*) impacts the structure of society itself. He explicitly states that "from the Christian vision of the human person there necessarily follows a correct picture of society" (13). This society of individuals and the families arising from the union of individuals, then, is prior to the voluntary formation of the state (cf. Locke, s. 77) whose power is inherently limited to two provisions (11):

1. Serving the instrumental function of coordinating all the social sectors or social institutions (such as the educational or the economic) to operate for the common good;
2. Providing for the protection of the rights of all individual members of the state.

Because society and the well-formed state depend so much on a correct understanding of the individual, John Paul devotes a lot of time in the beginning of the encyclical discussing the inherent and essential features of persons. This is important to his overall project in *Centesimus* because the individual is seen as the foundation of society and societal institutions; a proper understanding of the elementary nature of the individual provides a proper understanding, specifically, of economics and politics (46). "[W]hen hatred and injustice are sanctioned and organized by the ideologies based on them, rather than on the truth about the human person, they take possession of entire nations and drive them to act," waging wars and oppressing peoples (17). War and oppression are wrong precisely because they violate the rights of individuals (17).

The most fundamental characteristics upon which social institutions must be based are the freedom, autonomy, and rights of individuals. Since each person is a subject whose voluntary decisions and commitment build the social order, social institutions must be constructed in such a way that the good of the individual is realized with reference to his free choice (13). John Paul additionally maintains that the concept of the person ought not be construed as only a series of social relationships. Viewing persons as essentially "molecular," as only a part of a greater whole, dehumanizes the individual and denies the individual's fundamental autonomous nature as a moral agent (12–14).

The notion of freedom as expressed in the sections mentioned above, as well as in the entire encyclical, is a complex one. John Paul appears to sanction two distinct yet related aspects of this concept. In the first place there is what we label as "transcendent freedom." Since God created the person in his own image and likeness, he conferred upon all humans an essential dignity (11), which entails that persons were created for freedom (25). It is the nature of this transcendent freedom that it discover and obey the truth:

> The apex of development is the exercise of the right and duty to seek God, to know Him and to live in accordance with that knowledge. In the totalitarian and authoritarian regimes, the principle that force predominates over reason was carried to the extreme. Man was compelled to submit to a conception of reality imposed upon him by coercion, and not reached by virtue of his own reason and the exercise of his own freedom. This principle must be overturned and total recognition must be given to the rights of human conscience, which is bound only to the truth, both natural and revealed. The recognition of these rights represents the primary foundation of every free political order (29).

> The human person receives from God its essential dignity and with it the capacity to transcend every social order so as to move towards truth and goodness (38).

The *locus* of operation of this transcendent freedom is conceptions of reality. According to John Paul, a major problem with the regimes of Eastern Europe prior to 1989 was precisely that they imposed a view of reality that precluded every person's obligation to pursue knowledge of God and his will—the truth—through the free exercise of reason. Clearly the freedom to move toward and obey the truth applies univocally to each individual; in John Paul's view, it is a call to move beyond the social, cultural, economic, and political structures of the world. It expresses the distinctly "spiritual" obligation of humankind as distinguished from the "worldly" obligations we all have.

The other concept of freedom operative in *Centesimus* we call "practical" freedom, because it addresses those "worldly" obligations.

> All human activity takes place within a culture and interacts with culture. For an adequate formation of a culture, the involvement of the whole person is required, whereby one exercises one's creativity, intelligence and knowledge of the world and of people. Furthermore, a person displays his capacity for self-control, personal sacrifice, solidarity and readiness to promote the common good. Thus the first and most important task is accomplished within the heart. The way in which one is involved in building one's own future depends on the understanding a person has of himself and his own destiny (51).

Rather than transcending every social order, John Paul sees practical freedom as operating within the related realms of culture, society, economics, and politics. Practical freedom encompasses the range of choices individuals make regarding what opportunities they pursue, what employment they engage in, and what items they purchase—in short, all the choices that comprise how individuals function in the daily tasks of living. There are many ways in which one might express his concern for the other or promote the common good, for "it cannot be forgotten that the manner in which the individual exercises freedom is conditioned in innumerable ways" (25), including the "social structure in which one lives, by the education one has received and by the environment" (38). There is no transcending the social order here.

While specific cultures, environments, and social structures—if they are well-formed—derive their essential character from the truth as discovered from transcendent freedom, nonetheless the range of particular choices open to individuals in the sphere of practical freedom is incredibly wide and only limited by socially mediated and material factors.

We have spent some time developing this distinction because it is crucial for understanding precisely where the theological fault-line lies between John Paul's critique of liberalism, which some see as entailing its rejection, and the larger argument he makes in support of liberalism. It is precisely because these two notions of freedom are rendered indistinct or even conflated as a subtext in *Centesimus* that so much confusion about John Paul's views abound. While we will elaborate upon this problem in greater detail below, it is necessary to bear in mind that these two concepts are in tension throughout the encyclical, as they are in tension throughout the life of the church: the dual conception of freedom, one pertaining to theological issues and the other to worldly matters, provides a framework whereby Christians can simultaneously be "spiritually" disciples of Jesus and also pledge allegiance to the powers of the world. By using this phony distinction, the church can engage in risk-free religiosity: we can divide our loyalties in such a way that celestial demands have no bearing on terrestrial concerns such as our money, our lifestyles, or the specific material "common good" of our economic ideology.

In *Centesimus,* the fundamental confusion arising from the indistinctness of the dual concept of freedom is most telling in John Paul's discussion of rights. Even so perspicacious a reader as Stanley Hauerwas maintains

> In contrast to more recent encyclicals the liberal language of rights in *Centesimus* is distinctly muted. Certainly "rights" are still used to mark important goods, but the notion that rights are primary moral notions is clearly rejected (Hauerwas, 1995, p. 131).

While it is true that the exercise of transcendent freedom, as Hauerwas states, "is not an appeal to the right of a person to make up his or her own mind" regarding truth, nonetheless John Paul's discussion of rights throughout *Centesimus* is prominent, well-defined as so fundamental to his moral theory that they have no derivation and need no justification, and are crucial to the development of his liberal theory, especially regarding economics.

John Paul recognizes two classes of rights that directly correspond to the dual concept of freedom discussed above. This seems to make sense because, following John Paul's reasoning, if one is free to do something then clearly one has a right to do it. He states that there are rights one acquires through work (associated with practical freedom) and "rights which do not correspond to any work performed but which flow from one's essential dignity as a person" (11) (associated with transcendent freedom). John Paul's intention appears to be that this dual notion of rights function in a way identical to the dual notion of freedom: the universal nature of "transcendent" rights inform and provide the lens through which we come to understand the separate, more concrete, and work-related "practical" rights, which are delineated and defined by the specific conditions of one's workplace, or by the level of economic development of one's nation or geographic region.

If we consider, along with Hauerwas, that the way John Paul regards and treats the issue of rights is in some large measure indicative of his acceptance or rejection of liberalism, then, simply based on this hypothesis, *Centesimus* is not only fully consistent with liberalism but must be viewed as a liberal document. To give a few examples from the text, John Paul asserts that rights are inalienable and proper to the human person (7), that these natural rights precede the individual's membership in society (7), and that the requirement of transcendent freedom to discover and obey the truth entails respecting the rights of others (17). Further, he defines the God-bestowed dignity of the person not as something that exists separately of and prior to rights but in terms of rights themselves: "The root of modern totalitarianism is to be found in the denial of the transcendent dignity of the human person who, as the visible image of God, is therefore by his very nature the subject of rights which no one may violate" (44). Similarly, he describes the Holocaust as a violation of the most sacred human rights (17), and the overthrow of communist regimes in

Eastern Europe in 1989 as a move to liberate persons and affirm human rights (26).

This brief discussion is more than an attempt to fraternally correct Hauerwas's misreading of an important feature of *Centesimus,* or a purely academic exercise to try to understand the liberal basis of the pope's invocation of rights. John Paul's overall argument that inalienable human rights have a theological basis and are understandable in terms of the dignity conferred on persons by God, as well as his connection of this theological position with the more secular, philosophical view that rights are morally primitive, natural, and inalienable, has significant implications for the way he intends us to regard the right that is central to the primary focus of the encyclical.

While John Paul provides a veritable laundry list of human rights in sections 6–10, the inalienable right which is most prominent throughout *Centesimus* is the right of the individual to own private property. This right does most of the heavy lifting in the document. It is precisely in John Paul's sacralization of private property that he not only accepts but blesses market capitalism.

In his discussion of *Rerum Novarum,* John Paul reinforces the basic dignity of workers and work. It is interesting to note at this juncture that John Paul seems to think that all work is dignified because all workers have dignity, a connection which is tenuous at best and patently false in too many instances to enumerate. Yet he is able to do this because of his curious definition of "work," which he maintains is the procurement of "what is necessary for the various purposes of life, and first of all for self-preservation" (6). This duty to exert oneself in order to secure self-preservation encompasses the most basic and most general activity of working and is, therefore, fundamental to every individual. Further, John Paul includes within the concept of the duty of self-preservation the additional obligation for the ongoing development of the self. Thus, since every individual is obligated to preserve his/her own life and to continue to develop as a person, every individual not only has the obligation and right to work but also "to possess the things necessary for one's personal development and the development of one's family" (6). In short order John Paul establishes the natural human right (and obligation—so much for St. Francis of Assisi) to own private property, which he maintains is fundamental for the freedom, autonomy, and development of the person (30). By thus tying private ownership of goods to the most basic characteristics of persons, John Paul elevates and sanctifies private property to the status of a sine qua non and will use this right as the most vital premise in his argument in favor of market economics.

The elaborated justification that John Paul offers in the encyclical for private ownership is virtually identical to that made by John Locke in his *Second Treatise of Government* (especially s. 25–51) published in 1690 and rightly considered the central document in the development and philosophical justification of liberalism. * Indeed, John Paul's account is so similar to Locke's that one might be tempted to think that *Centesimus Annus* was promulgated not to celebrate the hundredth anniversary of *Rerum Novarum* but the three hundredth anniversary of the *Second Treatise*.

Locke's stated concern at the beginning of his chapter on property (s. 25) is to show how there could possibly be a natural individual right to private property since God had given the earth and all material things contained within it to all humanity in common. Locke reasoned that because every person has a natural right to preserve his or her life, God gave the earth to humanity in order to provide for our subsistence: "God, who hath given the world to men in common, hath also given them reason to make use of it to the best *advantage* of life and convenience" (s. 26, emphasis added). It follows, then, that each person has a natural right to appropriate what is needed to sustain his or her life. Locke's argument thus far only justifies the *use* of material goods rather than the private ownership of those goods. What he establishes in order to effect the transition from a right to use to a right to private ownership of property is the principle that every person has property rights to his or her own self and his or her own labor, which is the mixing of the self with a material good (s. 27). This, then, enables the individual to appropriate and claim as his own whatever commonly-

---

* Michael Novak (1993) sees "some affinity" between John Paul's account of private property and Locke's. Max Stackhouse (1991) notes that the Pope's discussion "sounds like" Locke's. Both of these commentators understate John Paul's debt to Locke.

held good he mixes with his labor. Thus we have the classical liberal account of the genesis of private property.

In addition, Locke also argued that there were three limitations to the amount of private property any individual could rightfully own:

1. Any individual may appropriate only as much material goods as leaves enough of equal quality for others (since everyone has the same natural right to self-preservation) (s. 27).
2. Any individual may appropriate only as much as he or she can use before it spoils, for "Nothing was made by God for man to spoil or destroy" (s. 31).
3. Any individual is entitled to appropriate as his private property only those goods with which he has mixed his labor (32).

If we now return to *Centesimus,* we can trace the identical argument. John Paul establishes the same problem as Locke:

> The original source of all that is good is the very act of God, who created both the earth and humankind, and who gave the earth to humankind, so that we might have dominion over it by our work and enjoy its fruits (Gen. 1:28). The earth, by reason of its fruitfulness and its capacity to satisfy human needs, is God's first gift for the sustenance of human life (31).

The key for sustaining life is work, and from our labor mixing with commonly-held goods arises the concept of private property:

> It is through work that we succeed in dominating the earth and making it a fitting home. In this way, one makes part of the earth one's own, precisely that part which one has acquired through work; this is the origin of individual property (31).

John Paul even follows Locke in asserting that individuals have property rights to their own labor when he quotes Leo XIII in *Rerum Novarum* 130, "The Pope [Leo] describes work as 'personal, inasmuch as the energy expended is bound up with the person-

ality and is the *exclusive property* of him who acts, and, furthermore, was given to him for his advantage" (6, emphases added).

All that is left for John Paul's analysis to reflect Locke's liberal
theory accurately and completely is the doctrine that individuals
have property rights to their own selves. While John Paul does
not use that precise language, he does state

> In our time, in particular, there exists another form of ownership
> which is becoming no less important than land: the possession of
> know-how, technology and skill. The wealth of the industrialized
> nations is based much more on this kind of ownership than on nat-
> ural resources (32).

Further, he describes work—to which, as we have seen, individuals have property rights—as the utilization of our intelligence
and the exercise of our freedom (31). At a minimum, then, we
are justified in claiming that John Paul recognizes that individuals have property rights in their knowledge, skills, intelligence,
and freedom. While we cannot claim with certitude that this doctrine amounts to an individual's property rights in the self, it is
hard to imagine that whatever may be left out of this list and is
properly a characteristic of the self would not be subject to the
same analysis. John Paul seems to confirm our view when he
states, "Humankind's principle resource is the person himself"
(32).

We find it exceedingly curious that John Paul—as well as the
Church from Leo XIII to Vatican II—would decide to enshrine the
ownership of private property as a basic, inalienable human right.
Especially in the contemporary philosophical and political milieu,
the concept of rights is a contentious one and its use in this encyclical may not accurately express the substance of the Catholic
Church's social teaching (Williams, 1992). In addition, we are not
sure that all the uses of "rights" are comprehensible. For example, John Paul speaks of "national rights" and implies the existence of geographical or regional rights (22) but does not give an
account of what these rights specifically are, how they can be
derived, or how they relate to human rights.

Yet, even granting a univocal, classical liberal understanding of rights that is also comprehensible (a rather generous assumption), it is not clear to us why John Paul needs to delineate ownership of private property as a right. The reason, he maintains, that individuals have a putative right to property, as we have seen, is to guarantee self-preservation and ongoing personal development. If he wishes to engage in rights-talk, it is perfectly understandable for him to maintain that self-preservation and continuous personal development are fundamental, inalienable human rights (though the concept of "ongoing personal development" is one that needs much more elaboration than John Paul offers in *Centesimus*). Having posited those two basic rights, he does not need to make the further claims that ownership of private property is a right, and ownership of private property is a fundamental, inalienable right. Rather, he could well follow a path indicated by traditional Catholic philosophy.

While we are not great fans of St. Thomas Aquinas and view the church's continuing overreliance on Thomism, neo-Thomism, and natural law with much chagrin, Aquinas does make available a useful distinction that any admirer of his, such as John Paul, could have used in a discussion of the concept of private property:

> Community of goods is ascribed to natural law, not that the natural law dictates that all things should be possessed in common and that nothing should be possessed as one's own: but because the division of possessions is not according to natural law, but *rather arose from human agreement* which belongs to positive law, as stated above (ST Q57, AA2, 3). Hence, the ownership of possessions is not contrary to natural law, but *an addition thereto devised by human reason* (ST Q66, AA3, 1).

The distinction that Thomas indicates in this passage (without recourse to a concept of rights) is that, whereas natural law demands that each individual act in such manner to preserve and prolong his life and, further, dictates that all fruits of the earth have been given to all humanity for the purpose of self-preservation, natural law does not stipulate the means by which this common property is to be distributed. Private ownership of goods is *one* way to achieve this end, and it is consistent with natural law, but other processes which preclude private ownership might also be consistent with natural law.

Thus, a more accurate way to state and rewrite John Paul's central concern in *Centesimus,* using Aquinas's distinction, is to maintain that while self-preservation and continuous personal development are basic human rights, the right to private property is not God-given but historically contingent. A legal right to private property exists in much of the world because of the development of economic thought and processes (cf. 22) and the sterling advice of the IMF. But the important issue is that each person has an obligation to preserve himself and ensure that others can satisfy their obligation to preserve themselves through the use of goods we all hold in common. A right to private property is, clearly, only instrumentally good—good, that is, only insofar as it promotes the good of all persons. It is interesting to note here that almost all of the Roman Catholic religious orders reject the notion that their members have a right to own property privately. Property is usually held in common and each member's needs are met through communal decision and action.

Interestingly, John Paul gives voice to something akin to the contingency of private ownership when he states:

> Moreover, humankind, created for freedom, bears within itself the wound of original sin which constantly draws persons toward evil and puts them in need of redemption . . . . The human person tends towards good, but is also capable of evil. One can transcend one's immediate interest and still remain bound to it. The social order will be all the more stable, the more it takes this fact into account and does not place in opposition personal interests and the interests of society as a whole, but rather seeks ways to bring them into fruitful harmony. In fact, where self-interest is violently suppressed, it is replaced by a burdensome system of bureaucratic control which dries up the wellsprings of initiative and creativity (25).

While we find the pope's declamation against burdensome systems of bureaucratic control ironic since he has unleashed the dogs of the Vatican against a large number of theologians and activist clerics during his tenure, there are several areas in this selection that merit closer examination.

The parallel construction in the second and third sentences indicates that transcending one's self-interest is good and remaining bound to it is evil. Indeed, the first sentence indicates that remaining bound to self-interest is a prime example of the original sin from which we need redemption. This "wound of original sin," self-interest, presents the human community with a problem since it places the self in opposition to all others, including God. This problem of self-interest conflicting with and overriding the communal interest has attracted a long series of political solutions, from the communist regimes of Eastern Europe to contemporary policies of land redistribution in South Africa. John Paul objects to all manner of political solutions to this problem because:

1. Political solutions are performed through violence since they compel individuals to act as though they hold communal interests primary.
2. Political solutions make politics a "secular religion" in that the political order believes that it can effect redemption through legislative means.
3. Political solutions are impractical because sound economic activity ("initiative and creativity") would cease.

Since the justification John Paul offers for the private ownership of goods is that it guarantees self-preservation and the ongoing development of the self, and since guaranteed self-preservation and ongoing personal development is paradigmatic for an individual's immediate (as well as long-term) self-interest, this passage hardly provides a ringing endorsement of a fundamental right. Rather, it seems that John Paul undercuts his position to a large extent by framing an argument which states that

- Human self-interest is an evil, and
- Human self-interest is also a reality with which historical processes as well as temporal politics and economics must contend, because

- Human self-interest can not be eliminated from society by force without serious consequences for societal life.

We are not sure why John Paul finds it necessary to give the state advice on how to maintain stability and order. Such advice seems to go beyond the duties of a chaplain and also appears to be unnecessary. Even a totalitarian politician like Pontius Pilate knew that he had to bend to the people's will some of the time to maintain stability, and such a tactic seems to be a hallmark of empires since the time of Rome. We are also puzzled by the fact that the pope is so taken with utilitarian concerns and values in this passage when he criticizes them soon after. But what disturbs us most is that John Paul accepts this diagnosis as an irremediable feature of human nature and does not echo the gospel by calling the people of God to transcend their self-interest and pursue the life of poverty (which means no private ownership) to which we are called. We do not advocate that the church use force to eliminate self-interest as the prime motivating factor in human behavior, if indeed it is. The church does not have that kind of power, and what power the church does possess is already abused. The church is, however, the body of Christ, and the message of Jesus is precisely that we are no longer enslaved to the wounds of sin but are redeemed. The church should be urging us and supporting us in our efforts to leave self-interest behind in favor of charity, humility, and obedience to the gospel. We do not need the pope telling us that we are irredeemably sinful and that self-interest is so ingrained in our character that overcoming it is well-nigh impossible. It is as though Moses came down from Sinai and, seeing the golden calf, shrugged his shoulders and said, "Well, the chosen people of God have always had this character flaw. Let's not offend them by pointing out they are called to be better." And if this gospel message does undermine the political order and destabilize states and economic processes, as we believe it does, then so much the worse for politics, states, and economics.

By placing such emphasis on private ownership of property as a basic human right, John Paul elevates temporal politics and economics to an exalted position and to a level he explicitly renounces—that of a secular religion that, by never placing self-interest in opposition to other values, effects salvation. Further-more, such an argument devalues the experiences of the early church (see, for example, Acts 2:42–47) and discounts those religious orders who profess a vow of poverty.

What, then, does it mean for the church to accept the account of rights, the right to private ownership of property and a person's property rights to the self? As we will discuss below, John Paul severely criticizes capitalism's tendencies to commodify all human needs, reduce employees to mere units of productive capacity, and regard persons purely as markets or potential sales. What he claims this does is violate the inherent, God-granted dignity of every person; it marginalizes and alienates persons and treats them instrumentally, i.e., as means to secure profitability or promote selfish ends, rather than treating all persons as ends in themselves (per Kant, if we wish to follow the pope's secular reasoning) or as children of God (per Jesus, if we wish to follow the gospel). Yet John Paul's extensive use of the idea of private property as the engine of his encyclical, and especially in extending it to cover the essential constituents of personhood if not personhood itself, is the height of commodification. The reduction of persons to property leads directly to the view of persons as resources, the employment of which is always instrumental and dehumanizing. By calling persons "resources," John Paul sounds like any vice president of operations at a Fortune 500 corporation. "Resources" may be utilized, stockpiled, bartered, bought, sold, or distributed much as one could do with a pile of bricks, and with as much consideration. By maintaining that working expresses the dignity of persons and ignoring the fact that many jobs in most of the world are demeaning, degrading, and oppressive, as well as centered on the provision of goods and services that are luxurious, superfluous, and wasteful, John Paul functions as a consecrated, transnational chamber of commerce president.

Regarding persons as essentially property is purely an economic concept and entails that humanity's primary interactions be regarded as economic ones. Further, it is an economic concept arising from a particular economic ideology, namely capitalism. This entails that the correct kinds of interactions to take place in humanity are defined by the theoretic tenets of market capitalism. Thus, not only are social problems made understandable as aberrations in the correctly functioning structures of market capitalism (or as acts performed by those individuals who do not fully understand capitalism), but also that the solutions to human problems are to be sought in capitalism as well.

These, indeed, are the dominant themes of *Centesimus*. Market capitalism is sanctified as natural and, in fact, God-given; individualism is raised to theological prominence; and the gospel demands to poverty, selflessness, community, communal ownership, sacrifice, denial, neighborliness, charity, and on and on fall by the wayside and are not even mentioned in the encyclical. (If they were, they would be seen as illicit limitations on capitalistic practices.) In accepting and justifying capitalism, the church not only assumes citizenship status but behaves as a *good* citizen, one that is useful and subordinate to the aims and goals of the economic order. The church's sanctification of capitalism asserts its role as capitalism's chaplain and serves economics well in putting us at ease when considering the power capital markets exert on our lives. Subsumed under the cloak of world liberalism, the gospel is made subject to the dominant powers and empires.

6

Church as Citizen, Church as Chaplain

Introduction

In the last chapter we focused on John Paul II's encyclical *Centesimus Annus* because of the widespread notice it received in both the popular and theological press. We are Catholics, after all, and have grown accustomed to the periodic emanations from Rome that shed old light on new issues. Nonetheless, our expectations were raised (however slightly) by reports that *Centesimus* recorded a signal moment in the contemporary Roman Catholic Church's social teaching in that Pope John Paul II was finally taking capitalism to task and holding it accountable for numerous social injustices. Instead, what we found was John Locke attired in cassock and surplice. Instead of a thoroughgoing critique of the present-day, dominating, global economic system—especially necessary since the fall of capitalism's only rival in the modern world—we found in *Centesimus* a very clear statement of the putative theological underpinnings of the current secular order and a declaration of the integral connections between liberalism and Christian theological reflections on the state and economics.

It occurred to us that perhaps John Paul II's encyclical suffered, at least in part, by being written for a global audience: that its structure, tone, and content was dictated more by the pope's pluralistic and general concerns than by what we see as the Church's more particular needs. It must be said that it is not terribly clear to us how casting the issue in this way gets the pope off the hook for the ultimately pagan economic views he espouses in *Centesimus*. Such is the nature of the Roman Catholic Church today that we must greet many of the enunciations from Rome with a faithful yet bewildered shrug and an excuse that does not quite fit the bill.

We decided that we needed to search for other voices in the Christian tradition, voices that would take a more distinctively Christian approach to the issue of the church's relationship to business and the global economy. We do not ascribe to the division of Christ's body into discrete parts. There is one church with different—though related—traditions. We recognize and celebrate that we as Catholics have been enriched, especially in the recent decades, by the theological reflections of our sister Protestant denominations, and have been refreshed by their somewhat more philosophically restrained discussions of discipleship, Scripture, and the modern world.

The Protestant churches are not organized or governed in the same way as the Roman Catholic Church. Because there are a number of separate Protestant denominations, each with its own rich theological tradition, we felt justified in our expectation of a variety of diverse and eclectic approaches to the question of economics, economic development, and business practices. We were gratified by the number of regional church conferences and the multiplicity of statements, documents, and reports issued by the national churches. But upon examination, we found little difference in form or substance at all among the major declarations of the Protestant churches over the past twenty years: they are similar in tone; strike many common concepts and themes; and even utilize the same language, interpretation and analysis of the same, presumptively authoritative, scriptural passages. Furthermore, those concepts, themes, structures, and interpretations also have significant analogs within the Roman Catholic documents.

That was the most disconcerting discovery: the documents of the Protestant denominations share most of the assumptions and arguments evidenced in *Centesimus* even though the Protestant statements are often advisory in character, are often directed to local congregations, and are, therefore, much more limited in scope than their Roman Catholic counterpart. As much as we hope and pray for ecumenical union in the Christian church, we were disturbed to find such a singleness of vision regarding the "sacred" character of contemporary market economics.

In the opening section of this chapter we will examine some of the most salient of these positions. Because the large number of Protestant statements on social justice are so repetitious, and because of the limited scope of our inquiry, we make no attempt at comprehensiveness. As valuable as such an exhaustive examination would be, it lies beyond the aims of this work. Our claim is that the positions we examine are typical of the major denominations and give an insight into how the Christian church has accepted its assignment as servant to the dominant secular social order. In the latter part of the chapter we will analyze how these theological and religious positions have been utilized and specifically applied within the sphere of "Christian" business ethics. In so doing, we will illustrate how the Christian church affected the transition from acquiescent citizenship to active chaplaincy.

The Church as Good Citizen

One might find it curious that we have framed our discussion of church citizenship thus far mainly in terms of John Paul II's theoretical economic foundations as expressed in *Centesimus Annus* rather than on his more overt political statements. This is even more curious considering that we agree with Richard John Neuhaus (1997) that *Centesimus* is primarily a political document, that is, more about society, of which economics is only a part. Yet we also do not believe that economics is so easily separable from politics or culture generally as John Paul asserts (39, 40). As the Lutheran Church in America expressed it in *Economic Justice: Stewardship of Creation in Human Community,*

Economic activity is embedded in the total life of a society. Relations of production and distribution reflect the prevailing patterns of power as well as the values by which a society lives. The mate-

rial allocation within a society are both an affect and a cause of the
basic character of that society (Stackhouse 1995, p. 430).

The capitalist economic system that is advocated and defended
in the church documents we've examined is an integral and essential part of political and cultural liberalism. No theorist, be she a
political scientist or church functionary, can advocate one without simultaneously advocating the other. There is an identity of
ideological roots and a complementarity of societal function that
link the various aspects of liberalism into an actual as well as a
theoretical whole. Therefore, when John Paul II and the major
Protestant denominations level their minor criticisms at some of
the deleterious effects of the capitalist economic system, those
criticisms must be viewed within the context of the Christian
church's prevailing attitude toward political liberalism and the
core values that undergird both the political and economic spheres.
In what follows, we will examine the support the churches give
to those core values of liberalism and demonstrate that this support relegates the church to the status of "good citizen" and con-
signs it to the cheering section of the sidelines. With this status,
the church is emasculated and can offer no alternative ways of
viewing life, nor propose with any credibility differing substantive notions of the good based on the gospel.

The World Alliance of Reformed Churches (WARC), in its document "Justice for All Creation" (1997), draws attention to the
role Calvinism played in the development of liberal theory:

> Reformed structures have contributed to the establishment of mod-
> ern democracy. The goal of democracy is not merely that all may
> vote, but that all people participate in basic decisions affecting their
> future. The economy should not rule people; people should regu-
> late the economy (http://warc.ch /23gc/sec2-e.html).

Similarly, the United Church of Christ, in "Christian Faith and
Economic Life" (1997), maintains the strong link between the
original Protestant Reformers and contemporary political democracy through the Reformers' rediscovery of and emphasis upon
the covenant tradition of the Hebrew Bible. In addition, this doc-

ument also connects the values of liberal democracy to economics in the same way as WARC—a feature of most of the documents of the Protestant churches:

> All people are called to participate in, and to share the fruits of, creation and redemption. Those economic conditions that thwart full participation or that generate inequality and injustice therefore are as odious as despotic rulers. Just as governments finally become the property of those who are governed, so the economy belongs to the people who through it are fed and housed and inspired to produce for the needs of their neighbors and for the well-being of the whole community.

> Economic democracy envisages an economic system in which all people participate and through which all are nurtured. It assumes basic economic rights and the exercise of those rights through widespread social participation (Stackhouse 1997, p. 458).

The *Oxford Declaration* of 1990 (Stackhouse, 1997), while not asserting that political liberalism has its roots in the Reformation, maintains that "biblical values and historical experience call Christians to work for the adequate participation of all people in the decision-making processes or questions that affect their lives" (para. 54). This document also makes the parallel connection, however, between liberal politics and market economics. It indicates that, just as the dispersion of political power helps guard against totalitarianism, so does the dispersion of economic ownership help to protect people from the dangers of monolithic, monopolistic practices, promotes the control of economic life by a wide section of the population, and reduces the marginalization of the poor (56–58).

The key elements of the Protestant viewpoint is that the good of the people is best advanced, first, through the dispersion of political and economic power, and, second, through the participation of the largest number of people in the political and economic decision-making processes. It goes without saying that the marginalization of the poor would be reduced by this program: if the poor had a greater share of economic ownership they would cease to be poor and, therefore, cease to be marginalized. What is not so clear is how this is to be achieved and what it really means.

Clearly one of the two major underlying features of the Protestant reflection on faith and economics is its focus on rights. The rights they speak of attach to all persons and include a right to a secure life, equitable treatment, participation in political and economic governance, an opportunity to earn a "fair" living, and the right to provide for their own welfare. As expressed, these rights appear to be *entitlements*—those goods that are due to persons solely because they are persons. These rights also indicate, however, *powers* that attach to individuals. The right to participate in governance, for example, conveys to persons the ability to decide what course of action a government or economic system takes. The right to provide for one's own welfare implies that the individual has the power to decide what is for her own good and also has the ability to satisfy that good.

It is important to note, however, that rights as powers are significantly different from rights as entitlements. Entitlement rights apply to all individuals equally, whereas power rights may differ in degree depending upon the status of the individual. The power right of an individual to decide what is for her own good and the ability to satisfy that good are constrained by the material conditions the right-holder finds herself in. For example, the decisions Bill Gates may make about his own good and his ability to satisfy it differ significantly in degree from the formally similar decisions of a school janitor: the latter simply does not have the power right to satisfy his desire to lunch at any Parisian restaurant tomorrow afternoon, though he may have the power to choose a tuna sandwich over meatloaf. Rights as entitlements and rights as powers have similar functions: they are mechanisms that attach to individuals in order to promote some measure of self-determination. But the conflation of the two is misleading in that it offers an idyllic and illusory picture of equality in the powers we possess, especially in economic status.

The similarity of the function of entitlement rights and power rights appear to intersect in some democratic institutions. According to some prominent, traditional political contract theorists (such as John Rawls, following the liberal interpretation of the covenant tradition underlying Thomas Hobbes' *Leviathan* and John Locke's *Second Treatise of Government*), we have all made an agreement, whether explicit or tacit, to follow the will of the majority as expressed in voting. The existence of rights within this context supposedly achieves several goals, each of which are assumed by the Protestant churches. As entitlements, rights ensure that each individual may express his or her own will in the decision-making process, and that no one deemed qualified by the rules of the voting process may be excluded from casting his or her vote. As power, rights ensure that each individual voter may define for himself or herself what "the good" means, i.e., each individual has the legitimate authority to make his or her own decisions about what the outcome of the process should be. In terms of politics, this is an incredibly naive view. In terms of economic processes, it is sheer fantasy.

In both spheres, the alternatives individuals may choose are constrained by the structure of the political and economic order: we are given a limited number of options from which to choose, and those options are determined, in large measure, by an intricate web of assumptions, implicit values, and unquestioned faith in the process. It is not at all clear in what sense our wills are our own when the political agenda is determined by political parties, when the values by which we supposedly decide are defined by political institutions, and when the individually conceived good must coincide with the good of the "will of the majority" in order to be realized. To maintain that an individual or group of individuals have the power to change the political order is foolish. It is our belief that a community may live its life differently than that mandated by the liberal state, but that requires community rather than a group of individuals, and a coherent view of what that life could be. In 1630, Massachusetts Governor John Winthrop delivered the sermon "A Model of Christian Charity," which elaborated on this point. Contrary to popular belief, for Winthrop and the Puritans the basic idea of success and fulfillment centered upon the formation and maintenance of a community marked by the workings of the Spirit rather than on the accumulation of personal wealth and political power (Morgan 1965, p. 92). Simply put, we seem to have lost the vision that would enable us to frame an argument similar to that of Winthrop. There are no alternatives to the current political system and the values that underlie it, and the one community that could frame compelling alternatives—the Christian church—is at the moment unwilling to do so.

The situation is even worse in terms of globalized economics. It isn't even clear that there is enfranchisement of any kind, let alone the mythic enfranchisement of voting rights in a liberal state. What may pass for the economic franchise is purchasing power, but the purchasing power that would make any difference at all to the structure, function, or outcomes of the economic system are limited to a few individuals in the northern hemisphere. We are even more at the mercy of the vagaries of economic institutions than we are subject to states: the number of states that must devise political and social policies to satisfy the requirements of the World Bank and IMF should give statists cause for alarm. And we wonder why more aren't disturbed when increasingly political and social policies in the developed world are devised to conform to the mandates of Wall Street and the other major financial markets. As politics becomes even more subservient to economics, even the illusion of power that we have under the contract view dissipates.

What is most pernicious in the church's analysis of these structures is the claim that individuals stand in an "ownership" relation to politics and economics. As we will examine more closely below, the concept that we "own" our political and economic systems directly contradicts the primary message the church wants to send: that we stand in a stewardship relation to creation. How stewards—those who are charged with caring for the property of another—come to be owners of that property passes beyond puzzling to the realm of errant nonsense. As we shall see, stewardship means embodying and acting on the will of another—God—and it makes no sense to speak of our rights to do what we will with what we "own" in that context.

Nonetheless, the concept that we own the government and economic system is prominent in these documents and serves the interest of the secular order well. Not only does supposed ownership reinforce the illusion that we actually have decision-making power over the functioning of politics and economics, it also implies that a well-functioning social institution works to our benefit no matter how the fiscal goods are distributed. The poor have no cause for complaint if "their" economic system generates great wealth for others and subsistence for them. Even though the poor have no money, simply the fact that they own some of the shares, as it were, of the system constitutes wealth and status: the fact that some shareholders receive dividends while others do not is more a function of the type of shares that are owned rather than a result of an unjust system. As the value of the system increases, so do the value of our shares, since we are all part owners. If we are owners, we can't exploit ourselves—we are merely working to improve the value of our own property, an extension of ourselves.

When the church adopts these bizarre images of universal power and ownership, it completely undercuts the position of the very people it is trying to help—the marginalized and the poor.

The documents' other major underlying feature is the duty or obligation that is correlative to basic human rights. This feature is encapsulated by the claim that our overall responsibility is to promote the common good. This notion of the common good includes the prescription that, in their political and economic activities, all Christians ought to promote equality, protect the interests of the powerless and future generations, safeguard the environment, and provide for the community's needs. In the words of the Presbyterian Church (USA):

> The doctrine of God's love teaches that we are created for *community*. Justice is a *community* concept.

> As it affirms our right to individual freedom, it equally affirms our corresponding responsibility for the good of the community as a whole. We are to manifest the basic solidarity that binds us into one family. We are not only to share our resources individually with one another; we are to help fashion institutions which foster justice and well-being in the community. . . . Each member is not only to be free to participate but is responsible to participate on behalf of the body. [Through productive work] we express our sense of individual dignity and contribute to the well-being of others. For Christians, our responsibility to others knows no geo-

graphical boundaries (*Christian Faith and Economic Justice,* 29.131–29.132).

It is interesting that the church documents focus on the dual matrix and correlation of rights and the common good as a means to secure a well-ordered and unified political and economic system. It is also interesting that neither the Protestant churches nor Pope John Paul II develop a substantive notion of what the common good actually is or what "social well-being" means. As the excerpt from the Presbyterian document shows—and all the documents we've examined concur in this feature—the common good and social well-being are defined in terms of the entitlements and powers expressed by rights.

According to the church documents, the obligation to promote the common good in the main pertains to the wider sphere of the *effects* of the decision-making process of the social group. That is, a morally legitimate process is one that works to the common benefit of all those affected by it. For example, a key feature of promoting the common good in the church documents involves the obligation to promote equitable treatment. But it must be noted that equitable treatment is not a unipolar concept, that is, we can not make a decision regarding the question of whether an individual has been treated equitably simply by examining the condition of one person. Equity pertains to the ways in which a number of persons are treated by a process. Any individual may claim that his right to equal treatment has been violated by some process, and our attention seems to focus on his claim alone. But even the invocation of the entitlement to equal treatment must be made vis à vis some other individual or group of individuals who have been treated better by the process while their initial condition was the same as the putative victim's. What is implicit in the rights claim must be explicit in the obligation: all persons affected by a process must be treated equally; the process must be indifferent to the persons affected; and this equitable treatment must promote the common good.

What disturbs us is not the idea that obligations and rights are correlative. That idea is quite old in the history of liberal thought. We are disturbed, rather, by our belief that the church has made a major and fundamental error in throwing its lot in with the structure implicit in all this talk of the "common good." By adopting the liberal ideology linking social obligations with rights and accepting the liberal conclusion that the common good is defined by the entitlements and powers expressed by rights, the church also accepts the conclusion that the common good is purely procedural. The good for persons is not the kind of thing that merits substantive discourse; it is merely what autonomous individuals decide it to be in a "fair" process of decision making. This is why the church documents place such emphasis upon equity, power-sharing, and universal participation; all the relevant social ills are definable in terms of aberrant processes and can be cured by the development (or the reestablishment) of procedural fairness.

It is true that most of the church documents provide a laundry list of rights that ought to be secured by politics and, even more specifically, economics. Often included in many of those lists are claims that economic activity ought to provide for the needs of individuals, such as adequate food and clean water, health care, and housing. It is as though the church believes that its brief catalogue of the enumerated basic needs common to all satisfies its responsibility to address the issue completely. A mention is sufficient. Yet the church documents are not at all clear about how these "entitlements" are to be provided, and imply joyously that the correct functioning of the markets in the economic system ought to satisfy the needs of persons throughout the world.

This is the key contribution of the church's analysis of economic justice, and it is incredibly barren. None of the church documents give an adequate discussion of what constitutes "needs" other than vague and abstract references to human dignity; they do not discuss who may decide what "needs" are in particular societies, nor, indeed, whether needs differ from culture to culture. For example, is the condition of the poorest in the United States directly comparable to the condition of the poorest in Indonesia? Is it analogous, or does it differ entirely if our understanding of poverty is relativized to the context in which it occurs? In other words, if the poorest in the United States are not as bad off as the poorest in Indonesia in that the former have some access to health care, clean water, etc., while the latter do not, how are we to assess the function of the system? Painfully, there isn't even a brief analysis of how "needs" are distinguishable from "wants" in differing cultural contexts: in what sense do Americans need automobiles or 401(k) retirement funds or jobs that pay $40,000 per year? And if those are needs, should we be striving to provide more automobiles to pedestrians in Mexico City, or are the "needs" of the postindustrial north simply the "wants" of the emerging markets of the south?

What the economic system ostensibly provides through its processes—and what the churches endorse uniformly—is opportunity. Yet the churches never ask whether the mere opportunity to provide for one's needs is a sufficient condition for a process to be "fair"; nor do they consider that an individual's or group's failure, given opportunity within a "fair" process, is possible, nor what that failure means for the process itself. The captivity of the church within this liberal ideal is complete.

For the Common Good

It is impossible for us to overemphasize how destructive this development is for the Christian church. By accepting the fundamental theoretical basis of political/social liberalism, the church finds itself committed to accept the contemporary manifestation of market economics as well as its view of the person, self-realization, consumption, and everything else that view implies. In other words, the church accepts its citizenship status in the liberal world by buying into the secular order's common language and common understandings. Once it becomes a good citizen, the church accepts the role and function that is assigned to it as a subject of the temporal powers in the same way that other social institutions whose legitimacy depends on their good citizenship—such as the World Bank, IMF, Princeton University, Daimler/Chrysler, etc.—accept their respective roles and function. For the church, that role is chaplaincy, and the chaplain church's function is to sanctify (among many other things) market economics and its various processes. What Michael Novak wrote about *Centesimus Annus* is equally applicable to the Protestant denominations, since all the Christian churches walk lockstep in agreement on economics:

> [*Centesimus Annus*] is the single best statement in our lifetime by
> the Catholic Church, or any other religious body, of the moral
> vision of a political economy such as that of the United States. That
> is why John Paul's diagnosis of serious faults in such systems is not
> offensive; his criticism hoists us on our own ideals. It is, so to speak,
> criticism "from within". . . . In *Centesimus Annus* Rome has assim-
> ilated American ideas of economic liberty (Novak 1992, p. 142).

We agree with Novak that the chaplaincy church does indeed
criticize and exhort the powers of the world from inside its ideological tent, yet Novak is wrong when he states that Rome has
assimilated American ideas of economic liberty. Novak is clearly
alluding to the church's practice of christianizing pagan feasts and
rituals throughout its history—attempting to turn pine trees into
symbols of Jesus' birth on a day that pagan Rome delineated as
Saturn's birthday, for example. Rather, the American liberal, capitalist ideology has coopted and subjugated Rome and the other
Christian denominations. The American idea is paganizing Christian feasts, rituals, and images, and doing so with the church's
enthusiastic cooperation.

As we indicated above, the church cooperates with the secular
powers by adopting the secular notion of the common good. Some
theologians have read the church documents as much more dis-
paraging of capitalism and general business practices based on this
notion of the common good than we believe is justified. David
Schindler (1996), to cite one example, writes that while John
Paul II "endorses the economic freedom and creativity characteristic of a market economy, [he] nonetheless does so in the context of a carefully qualified criticism of capitalism" (115–16).

What the Christian church attempts to do is modify capitalism's
advocacy of the private ownership of property with a notion of
the common good. In other words, the church tries to make the
case that the accumulation and use of private property within the
context of market economics is justifiable just as long as the good
of all persons is advanced by such activity. The scriptural foun-

deducted. That such an approach gives primacy to capital owners is obvious, but it is not obvious what justifies this way of thinking about economics. Yet even if we grant the myriad of assumptions inherent in this view, none of the authors explain how
deriving profits in this manner is to be distinguished from profits
derived from exploitation, either in the form of charging high
prices to consumers or by paying low wages to laborers—assum-
ing that we already know what constitutes fair pricing and fair
wages. In fact, the doctrine may have the perverse effect of justifying such exploitative activities: if profit making is mandated
along with the universal destination of goods, then one could
argue that paying whatever counts as impermissibly low wages
or charging impermissibly high prices is not immoral at all. The
corporate executive is generating greater economic activity
through the profits earned—(maximally) satisfying the interests
of the shareholders and perhaps even the national economy while
(minimally) satisfying the interests of consumers and workers—
and the money is not really wrongfully appropriated since it will
eventually devolve back to the exploited (or their heirs). In fact,
exploitative business practices may be viewed as the ultimate
investment plan, so much better than a 401(k) since the exploited
will avoid the state's tax burden. That burden will be borne, generously, by the owners of the capital that makes it all possible.

By taking the perspective of the primacy of the capital owners
as a starting point, the requirement of securing profitability serves
to negate the counterclaims of consumers and employees: it is
only necessary that there be *some* distribution of the benefits of
economic activity. This criterion is so weak that it is hard to imagine what kinds of business activity would be excluded or what
kinds of business practices would be wrong. While all the church
documents talk about and mandate that the benefits of economic
activity be shared, none describes what constitutes a fair distribution of those benefits nor what "sharing" means. It is not even
clear to us that profits *per se* ought really to be included in what
is distributed, for it is possible that a fair distribution is achieved
simply by the exchange, for example, of labor for wages as determined by the local labor market. Certainly from the perspective
of capital owners, the benefits of economic activity are distributed

to all who participate in the business system as owner, consumer, or worker, and that distribution is fair as long as the current system is maintained, for all will benefit according to the impersonalized forces of the markets governing all aspects of the system.

This perspective certainly seems to satisfy the Christian churches' mandate, expressed by John Paul that the role of business is to promote the common good and operate "at the service of the whole of society" (34), but it is not clear that these utterances function as anything other than mere shibboleths. Indeed, even if they could be read substantively as a gospel-based critique of current business practice—and we are puzzled as to what, precisely, that would amount to given the context of the documents—it is just not evident that market capitalism is the best way, let alone the Christian way, of achieving those ends.

One of the other major problems with John Paul's discussion of profits in *Centesimus Annus* and with the other denominations' statements regarding profits is that no one gives any satisfactory indication of just how much profit is justifiable as a return on investment. Should justifiable profits be tied to some independent indicator, such as the average return on investment in a particular sector, on money market rates, or on some other index? The Evangelical Lutheran Church in America offers a guideline that is singularly puzzling. Its document on justice states that "the holder of wealth-producing property is entitled to a reasonable return as determined contextually by the society."

Part of what makes this guideline so unsatisfactory is that what may be considered "reasonable" depends on the initial perspective one adopts regarding the notion of private property. For example, granting the primacy of market economics, it is reasonable that private, for-profit enterprises like pharmaceutical companies secure a return on their investment proportional to the desire of consumers for their product. From the alternative standpoint of granting primacy to social welfare, it is just as reasonable to require that the needs of the ill and infirm be met without regard to their ability to pay. It is not reasonable, given our current social context, to expect that each of these "reasonable" perspectives can be satisfied simultaneously.

Further, as we indicated above, it is not at all evident that what is "reasonable" yields anything different than the principle "whatever the market will bear." Contemporary economic theory defines "reasonable" in precisely these "mutual" terms; to set profit margins artificially, i.e., to utilize factors other than the interplay of supply and demand, is to place unreasonable and debilitating constraints on economic activity. It is much more reasonable to allow market forces to moderate the system towards "equilibrium" and "fairness."

Finally, the reference to "society" is so vague that it is useless. What entity constitutes the society that provides the context for reasonableness is open to all sorts of "reasonable" interpretations, from groups of investors to local communities, to nation states, to the G8's interconnected money markets, to the global community. Any of these social groupings may satisfy the criterion, and the contextualization will shift accordingly.

The only thing that is clear from the churches' discussion of profits is that the holders of wealth-producing property are entitled to some measure of profit from the use of the goods they own. As we implied above, a more fundamental problem remains with the viewpoint the churches present, no matter how we resolve the questions of what constitutes fair profits or how economic benefits are to be distributed. It simply is extremely difficult to understand how one who legitimately owns private property and who is therefore entitled (if not required, by the churches' argument) to use that property to generate profits (at least some of which rightly belongs to the owner), could *simultaneously* consider those goods not as her own but as commonly held. There is a noxious logic here that defines "privately owned property" as common to all. Ostensibly, the churches are trying to have it both ways, and in so doing are being dishonest. Substantively, the churches have thrown their lot in with the secular powers, and in so doing have sold out the gospel.

What is the result of all of this? The Christian churches maintain a doctrine of rights and exalt especially the right to self-determination and the right to ownership of private property. Further, they maintain that the way these rights operate will ensure the development and maintenance of the common good. But none of the churches explains with anything resembling clarity how the exercise of this system of rights by individuals correlates to the system of obligations these same individuals have, nor how the interaction of rights ineluctably leads to the promotion of the common good. The churches imply that as long as participation in economic activity is open and available to all—in other words, as long as the procedures are "fair"—the common good will be achieved. Social justice is reduced to an "equitable" distribution of economic opportunity wherein all individuals may exercise their freedom in meeting their own needs, achieve self-determination, and thereby (somehow) contribute to the well-being of the community.

This is merely the acceptance of market economics and its status quo. The structure and language of the prevailing economic system is adopted. The process is the same. The results are the same. The churches give us no reason to challenge the economic system that exploits the poor and dominates all of us, nor do they give us sufficient reason even to modify the "natural" play of market forces that reduce us to data points, units of productivity, and indexes of consumer activity. On the contrary, the churches sanctify capitalism and encourage its growth and domination through their urging of equal opportunity for all nations. In their view, the only thing wrong with capitalism is that it has not been embraced quickly enough to enable all people to satisfy their appetites.

Capitalism promises to promote the common good, and the churches have adopted that promise. The fundamental notion behind this promise is very simple: the satisfaction of self-interest—those desires we have that are self-determined. The argument that flows from this simple construct is based on the idea that the substantive good for all people is impossible to define objectively with any accuracy. A plurality of people means that there is a plurality of goods such that "good" is not univocal. We can speak abstractly of the "basic necessities," but what that means concretely will vary greatly from community to community. For example, "decent housing" will have different descriptions in New York, Costa Rica, and Indonesia. Further, as Novak explains (1989,

1999), it is extremely difficult for any individual to know whether a decision she makes will ultimately be in her own interest; how very near impossible it must be to know what decisions will advance the good of others when we operate in so much ignorance about what their interests are.

Identifying the common good with the pursuit of self-interest appears to solve a myriad of social, political, and economic problems for both the ruling elites and the churches who are their acolytes. This identification provides the context within which we can understand the enumerated rights contained in church documents and in national constitutions. In this context, all rights boil down to the fundamental right of self-determination understood as providing for noninterference on the part of social structures in the decision-making abilities of equal individuals. It is clear, so the churches argue anyway, that this self-determination does not equate with selfishness. In order to secure one's long-term self-interest, one must maintain relationships and sustain cooperation over a long span of time. One must cultivate and practice the virtues of friendship, honesty, and trust. In short, each and every one of us must ensure that all the participants in an economic enterprise realize a benefit from that enterprise. They go on to maintain that in reality and contrary to appearances, economic activity in all the forms that business presents cannot ultimately be a zero-sum game in which one participant's gain comes at the loss of another. In order to maintain one's own interest (which is primary), we must guarantee that all derive some kind of benefit through a system of mutual and cooperative business activity. The rising tide of wealth that results will raise all boats, and everyone's self-determined good will be realized through the self-determined means within the system.

The expression of this doctrine over the past twenty years by the Christian churches is nothing but a reiteration of Adam Smith's invisible hand (as Novak admits, 1993, p. 105) conjoined with Jeremy Bentham's brand of utilitarianism. But neither Smith nor Bentham dressed up this classical market theory in the vestments of religion and spiritual purpose. The times have changed. With the obvious "success" of market capitalism as it metastasizes throughout the world, both Stackhouse (1995) and Novak (1999) argue that the true paternity of capitalism lies deep in the medieval European economy, identifying the monasteries in their productive capacity as proto multinational corporations. It is as though the Rule of St. Benedict was the forerunner of the Chicago School. It isn't enough for the churches to adopt and bless contemporary capitalism; we have to claim credit for it too.

From Smith and Bentham to Friedman and Rawls in this century, the prevailing argument of secular theorists is fully consistent with the major assumption of theological reflections on justice: it is improper to give a substantive definition of the common good. The liberal value of pluralism operating within fair procedures demands the priority of the right over the good. The system of domestic and global markets exists and is justified in its theoretical formulations precisely because interests are posited to be personal dispositions that are, and must be, self-defined. Goods and services are produced and distributed by corporations not by magic, philanthropy, or transcendent insight but by the demands of the consuming market. Prices are set not by the inherent value of the products but by what the consumers will pay. Wage rates are determined not by the value added by the workers nor by their skills but by what amount employees will be willing to work for. There is neither inherent value nor spirituality nor the gospel in this system but rather so-called "rational" agents pursuing their own self-determined, rationally chosen individual goods that the various markets endeavor to meet. Promotion of the common good, then, becomes easy to assess: one need only calculate the sum of satisfied individual interests. If that sum is greater than 50 percent, then the common good is achieved; if less, then the common good is frustrated.

The Christian churches abandon the field to market economics by not providing a substantive alternative to this dominant, secular notion of the common good. They abandon their responsibility by not discussing how their alternative can be best achieved, or, indeed, whether there is any value in the concept of the common good in the first place. Their pleas for the poor beg the question of the adequacy of market "solutions" to poverty by complaining that the mechanism is not fully available. Instead of analyzing and critiquing the notions of individualism, common good, self-determination, and self-interest, the churches accept them as givens. In so doing, the church accepts a complete inversion of reality.

Are our interests really our own? Are we truly able to determine our selves and our fates rationally and independently in the way the churches assume? The modern corporation spends hundreds of billions of dollars annually in various blatant and subtle forms of advertising that create or redirect our desires for the products and services the corporation produces. Multinational corporations do not satisfy our needs; we satisfy theirs. We desire faster computers, sportier cars, and sleeker sneakers simply because they are produced and because we believe that we are less without them. Globally, the American economic/consumer dream is reproduced and emulated, even in nations that are ostensibly anti-American.

We have made a fetish of having. The fetish for the newer, faster, bigger, and shinier is not in our self-interest. It is expensive and wasteful to upgrade, buy new software, sign a lease for a Lexus, or purchase a Versace ensemble. It takes more work and the hours work consumes to pay for those things, and our dependence on our jobs and the goodwill of our employers grows proportionately as we have more goods to support by our work. Our debt load and anxiety increases, and the economists and government experts label this phenomenon "consumer confidence," without which the system suffers. Those who benefit from this system are the corporations themselves. They have created, with our complicity, the dominating values of our global culture from which we are too blind, weak, and afraid to deviate. And our church, which has the resources to stand against this leviathan, can't even give an adequate expression of needs.

If the myth of self-determination that the church buys into weren't enough, the idea touted in the social justice documents that the capitalist system yields social cooperation through an end to both selfishness and zero-sum games is laughable. Someone—and here we are talking about many millions of people—loses every day so that the system can be maintained and some others may benefit. So much has been written and so little heeded about slave laborers in China producing Barbie dolls for our little girls, the exploitative conditions in the *maquiladoras* of northern Mexico producing cheap motherboards for personal computers, child labor throughout the Pacific Rim, migrant workers imported from the Caribbean basin to harvest American fruit and vegetables for pennies a bushel, the Thais and Hondurans working in sweatshops manufacturing Kathy Lee Gifford clothing. The list of horror, abuse, disease, and death goes on and on to the point where it ceases to appall us. There certainly is cooperation in our global economy, but it is the cooperation born of poverty and despair. The exploitation of the poor is fully justified by the system: the self-interest of the poor is satisfied because they are kept alive in order to come to work tomorrow. The horrible working conditions aren't really that bad since they are the means by which the poor's basic needs can be satisfied, and without that, they would die more quickly. Besides, if we allow the system to work naturally and remove trade barriers and minimum wage requirements, it's only a matter of time before the cost of labor will reach equilibrium and the huge differential in the earning power between workers in the northern hemisphere and workers in the southern will meet somewhere in the middle.

Of course the church has decried these conditions. Of course the church laments over the fate of the poor and the vulnerable. But the church also refuses to see these conditions and this fate as mandated by the economic system, demanded and created by the fundamental determinations of the global economy. The church deludes itself that these are merely "aberrations" and "excesses" of an essentially just process. But rational consumers choose cheaper products. Cheap prices (and high profits) demand cheap production costs. Cheap production costs requires cheap labor, and no one works more cheaply than those who are facing starvation and have no other choice. Capitalism requires the exploitation and commodification of people in myriad ways in addition to these examples from the labor markets. The rising tide will raise all boats, but it will also swamp the swimmers and drown those treading water.

Even for those of us who have boats, who are well-off in comparison to the billions of people in the developing world, the system is degrading, first and foremost because we reap what we do not sow in enjoying the products others die to produce. We don't have to see the child laborers, so they do not have to exist for us and we can go on merrily shopping for the cheapest prices. Our convenience and comfort is measured less by the size of our VISA bills and more by the poverty we engender. We are degraded by our self-satisfaction. The U.S. economy has been booming during the last twenty years because of gains in productivity. Our economy will continue to flourish only as long as our productivity increases, and isn't that a wonderful thing born of the new technology? Yet the reality behind productivity gains is not simply the computerization of the workplace; it also includes the fact that fewer workers have to work harder for longer hours to produce more without concomitant gains in income and benefits. More goods and services are good for the economy, but increases in wage rates are inflationary and dangerous for the system—that is, except for corporate executives who could make stock prices rise. They are worth whatever obscene amounts of money we can throw at them because they raise stock prices through increased efficiency, also very good for the system. The stock price of an already highly profitable AT&T in 1998 rose to new heights at the announcement of forty thousand employees losing their jobs. The market loves restructuring, layoffs, outsourcing, on-demand employment, and decreases in employer provided health benefits because the companies' profits rise as expenses fall. And because so many employees' retirement benefits are invested in the stock market, we see the peculiar phenomenon that what's good for the workers is that workers be exploited, discounted, and discarded. The American worker is consuming herself and calling it nourishment.

Nor is this all. We believe that the church's acceptance of the basic principles of liberalism and market economics also affects its self-understanding. It is nearly impossible to sacralize contemporary corporate business structures and the economic system that undergirds them to the extent the church does without adopting their attitudes and behavior. To a large extent it seems that the church has come to view itself as a worldwide corporate institution analogous to Microsoft, even to the extent of adopting some of that company's litigation strategies.

For example, it is no secret that there are a surprising number of Roman Catholic dioceses in the United States and Canada that are facing severe financial difficulty or even bankruptcy because of pending civil lawsuits alleging the sexual abuse of children by priests. Many bishops in these dioceses stand accused of complicity in that, once informed of a priest's illicit behavior, the bishops apparently decided to "solve" the problem by transferring the priest to a different parish church. Frequently, neither the priest nor his victims received psychological counseling.

Edward Cardinal Egan, Archbishop of New York, was involved in this situation during his tenure as Bishop of the Diocese of Bridgeport, Connecticut. In that diocese, at least thirty people have accused eight priests of pedophilia and have also accused Egan and his predecessor of knowledge of the problem and of shuffling the priests from one parish to another in an attempt to cover it up. Confronted with these lawsuits, Egan developed a legal defense in his deposition that is a novel one for the Church, though a standard one for American corporations. Egan argued that priests are independent contractors and, therefore, the diocese is not liable for their actions (Goodstein, 2000). Eventually the Diocese of Bridgeport reached a settlement with the thirty victims.

There is so much that is disturbing and reprehensible about this example. We don't know how effective Egan's strategy was since the notion that priests are independent contractors was never tested in court. Nor do we know whether this position affected the litigants' decision to settle the suit. We do know, however, that subsequent to Egan's deposition he was promoted to the archbishopric of New York and then made cardinal. It is obvious, though, that Egan, arguably the most prominent Roman Catholic cleric in the United States, has a conception of the Church that makes it just another corporation among corporations, without conscience, denying guilt and responsibility especially if guilt and responsibility affect the bottom line.

7

Toward an Economics of Discipleship:
The Church as *Oikos*

Introduction

If the Christian church is to be something other than a chaplain
to the powers of contemporary capitalism, several profound
changes in its self-understanding are needed. It must cease redefining the Christian mission into terms compatible with capitalist
ideologies and techniques. It must no longer tolerate the exploitation of Christian cultural resources by firms, states, and others
whose actions deepen the hold of instrumentalist approaches to
faith and Christian practice. It must, in other words, reverse those
patterns of thought and practice that render the church incapable
of critiquing capitalism or the modern state in any significant
sense.

   If the church as chaplain is a bad idea, as we believe, the alternative is for the church to take itself more seriously as a polity in
its own right—not a functionary or lackey of existing institutions
or powers but an alternative community called by God to model
a distinctive way of being in the world. New Testament scholar
Richard Hays refers to this vision as one that sees the church as
God's "demonstration plot" (Hays, 1996), while many others use
language describing "the church as *polis*." This increasingly popular notion, highlighted in recent years by Stanley Hauerwas and

others, represents an important but largely underdeveloped category useful in saving the gospel from the killing embrace of Christianity Incorporated.

Indeed, a strong notion of "the church as *polis*" undergirds much of our argument. Instead of a church that effaces its particularity and the demands of the gospel (in order to be supportive of the national project, the dominant economic ideology, or the requisites of business), we want the church to "recenter" the gospel as the primary source of allegiances and identity for Christians in our day. The church as the "first family" of Christians (Clapp, 1993) delegitimizes the strongest claims of state, class, family, and ideology; it calls and forms a people bound by mutuality, forgiveness, and peaceableness instead of selfishness, division, and coercion. In this sense, the church as *polis* is not a counterculture in the narrow sense of being defined primarily in opposition to the norms of a dominant culture; rather, for Christians the church ought to be the *true* culture of the kingdom of God, a people gathered to experiment with ways of living as if the kingdom had already begun its reclamation of the world.

The vision of the church as the true polity for Christians in the world has helped illumine many areas of theological ethics and church life—militarism, racial and gender exclusions, socialization processes, and more. But while the image has been a helpful corrective to accommodated theologies that enable Christians to kill other Christians (and anybody else), it has less frequently been employed in trying to situate matters of discipleship and economics. And if the *polis* the church is meant to be is to be anything more than a pious metaphor, it must explore how capitalism aids or inhibits the making of disciples and the exemplary quality of the church. If taking the body of Christ as one's primary identity undermines the easy justifications of Christians killing one another in wartime, how does it assess the myriad forms of coercion and exploitation—sometimes with lethal consequences—that are unremarkable features of practices formed by capitalist institutions and worldviews in which Christians are willing participants?

For the church to be a real-world alternative to the coercive nature of the modern state and contemporary capitalism, the "church as *polis*" metaphor needs to be completed by the development of the "church as *oikos*" ("household," the Greek root for economy), oriented to the kingdom of God as proclaimed and exemplified by Jesus.

In Aristotelian thought, a healthy *polis*, or political community, required certain structures of economic organization supportive of the proper ends of political life. These practices centered on the household (or *oikos*); differences in *polis* or *oikos* made for different types of societies and ways of life.

Just as the radical Christian reappropriation of the polity imagery does not presuppose commitment to Aristotle's particular list of proper political ends, so too asserting the need for the church to itself be an economic *oikos* does not entail the Aristotelian assertion that households should organize the labor of women and slaves in ways that liberate the male head of the household to participate fully in politics. What the Aristotelian pairing of the two does is remind the church that being its own polity (rather than an adjunct to some more central polity like the state, clan, or racial group) *necessarily* presupposes a set of economic practices, ideas, and relationships supportive of the proper ends of the church, which is the kingdom of God as it unfolds in human history.

Given the limits of this book, we can only highlight some considerations and areas of inquiry that might contribute to a more coherent "economics of discipleship." Doing so might encourage others to experiment with plans and practices that enable the church to live more completely according to the priorities and practices of Jesus rather than by the celebration of the powerful found in Christianity Incorporated.

The Economics of the Sermon on the Mount

The Sermon on the Mount (Matthew 5–7) may simultaneously be the best-known part of the Gospels, if not the entire Bible (e.g., Harrington, 1998), and among the most contested parts of the Christian experience. It joins together the upside-down blessings of the Beatitudes, the Lord's Prayer, the "Lillies of the Field," and the Golden Rule. It contains the most important "hard sayings" of Jesus—to love one's enemies, to repay evil with good, to put aside material worries, and to rejoice in persecution and suffering. It is simultaneously a key to the entire Christian movement—Augustine called it "a summary of the whole gospel," and Pope John Paul II describes it as "the Magna Carta of Gospel morality"—and a call to practices that most Christians in most of history have sought to avoid (Dumais, 1998, p. 316; *Veritatis Splendor*, 1993, No. 15).

In mainstream Christianity, this evasion has at least two primary variants. An influential Protestant version derived from Martin Luther sees the Sermon as an impossible ideal, the pursuit of which brings Christians to a failure so powerful that the sinner's heart finally opens to God's grace. The Catholic variant holds that the Sermon is normative only for the minority of Christians called by God to an intensified degree of discipleship (traditionally in a religious order); the majority of baptized Christians, by contrast, need only to conform their conduct to the Ten Commandments and the dictates of natural law informed by the church's teaching (for one expression, see Dumais, 1998, p. 318). Contemporary expressions of these approaches can be seen in luminaries including Reinhold Niebuhr and John Courtney Murray.

Still another evasion tactic undermines the importance of the Sermon (not to mention the rest of the Jesus movement) by claiming that Jesus and his earliest followers expected the culmination of the kingdom in their immediate future. Since the antirational practices of the Sermon were intended as an "interim ethic," and since we now see such an immanentist eschatology as flawed, the Sermon should not be seen as a guide to conduct in our time of delayed eschatology.

Critiques of the ecclesiology, hermeneutics, and eschatology undergirding these positions are abundant (see for example Harrington, 1998; Wright, 1996; Cahill, 1994). Approaches like these that evade the radical imperatives of the Sermon simultaneously remove the particularities of the priorities, practices, and dispositions of Jesus in the Gospel narratives, to be replaced with the conventional wisdom of any given age. In our day, avoiding the Jesus of the Sermon—and replacing him with the Jesus of corporate management, for example—is an essential step in fashioning Christianity Incorporated. To resist the chaplaincy role provided for the church in our time means reappropriating the Sermon on the Mount as a constitutive feature of Christian life and practice.

Of course, the Sermon maintained such a status for various groups in Christian history (and for much of the church in the pre-Constantinian era)—from the monastics to the mendicants, the Anabaptists to the Catholic Worker movement. The Sermon has been primarily influential among such renewal movements for its teaching on nonresistance and violence—matters central to how Christians should approach war and killing as political practices (Cahill, 1994). Substantially less attention has been devoted to the *economic* implications attendant to radical discipleship as framed by the Sermon (an illustrative exception is Heilke, 1997).

As one point of entry into the economics of discipleship, or of considering the church as *oikos,* we now turn briefly to the Sermon for glimpses into themes, aims, and criteria that could inform the church's economic vision and practice. While one cannot read off a set of comprehensive economic imperatives from the Sermon, it can provide a valuable starting point in thinking about economic practices commensurate with ecclesial identities and mission grounded in the Sermon's call to radical discipleship.

Intensifying and Deepening the Law (Matt. 5:17–48)

The Jewishness of Matthew's Jesus runs throughout the apostle's narrative—far from abrogating the law, Jesus intensifies, deepens, and expands the law's best sense at every turn. With the kingdom having broken through in the person and proclamation of Jesus, the law's concessions to human limitation and sin are removed. With the Messiah here and the Holy Spirit to follow, followers of Jesus' Way have all the help required to begin living the law's best intent without reservation, without appeal to loopholes, without evasion.

Where the law prohibited murder, Jesus now proscribes anger and nursing a grudge. Jesus extends the ban on adulterous conduct to include adulterous and possessive desire. Divorce, oath-taking, revenge, and conduct with enemies—it is as if Jesus puts the law on a diet of steroids and growth hormones to make its impact more powerful than ever before. So powerful is the Spirit of God, so decisively has the kingdom of God arrived, that God's true desires for humanity can now be pursued without dilution—straight, no chaser.

This pattern of the law not being abolished, but rather intensified by Jesus and the imperatives he lays on his followers, provides a starting point for any economy of discipleship. By any measure, the law's conception of covenant and justice dealt with economic matters as primary concerns. The examples the Sermon provides of Jesus' approach to the law—to radicalize it and see its manifestation among his disciples as testimony of and contribution to the inbreaking kingdom—describes the pattern into which Israel's economic practices are situated.

Israel's economic practices and ethics have been explored usefully by scholars from multiple disciplines in recent years. For our purposes, Ched Myers' description (1998) of the Sabbath as the key to Israel's notion of divine economy is helpful. Sabbath originates in Genesis as a time following the good work of creation. Humans are to imitate God in practicing Sabbath, the full implications of which only begin to take shape in the Exodus accounts of liberation, flight, and Israel's radical dependence on Yahweh. Unlike the imperial Egyptian economy, which produced abundance for some via extortionate policies aimed at the weak, Yahweh institutes an economic regimen of sufficiency, inclusiveness, and trust.

As Myers notes, the manna story is much more than a simple feeding miracle. In fact, "It is a parable that illustrates Yahweh's alternative to the Egyptian economy." Yahweh's instructions on how to gather manna constitutes "the people's first lesson outside of Egypt," and it is a lesson in economic production. The people are instructed to gather enough bread—not too little and not too much—so that none were deprived or overstocked. Further, this bread was not to be stored up—as Myers notes, power in Egypt derived from economic surplus and the political domination it both presupposed and empowered. Indeed, "It is no accident that Israel's forced labor [in Egypt] consisted of building 'store cities' (Exodus 1:11) into which the empire's plunder and the tribute of subject peoples was gathered." Rather than accumulating wealth, Israel is ordered to redistribute it—and trust that Yahweh's generous abundance will yet provide adequate bread the next day.

Finally, the Israelites were ordered to collect a double ration on the sixth day, in order to observe Sabbath on the seventh. Far from being a quaint recommendation on rest or leisure, Myers sees Sabbath as "the beginning and end of the law":

> Torah's Sabbath regulations represent God's strategy for teaching Israel about its dependence on the land as a gift to share equitably, not as a possession to exploit. . . . The prescribed periodic rest for the land and for human labor means to disrupt human attempts to "control" nature and "maximize" the forces of production. Because the earth belongs to God and its fruits are a gift, the people should justly distribute those fruits, instead of seeking to own and hoard them.

The Sabbath extends to the land itself later in Exodus (23:10–11), as an injunction to leave the land fallow every seventh year. The Sabbath extends to debt release in Deuteronomy (15:1–18), and most notably in the Levitical Jubilee (Lev. 25). Debts are to be forgiven every seven years, creditors are forbidden to tighten credit in the years before Sabbath release, and a thoroughgoing Jubilee is to be practiced every "seventh-Sabbath"—or every 49 years. This latter restructuring aims

> to dismantle structures of social-economic inequality by: releasing each community member from debt (Leviticus 25:25–42); returning encumbered or forfeited land to its original owners (25:13, 25–28); freeing slaves (25:47–55) (Myers, 1998).

By restraining the urge to amass wealth and translate that wealth into domination (the Old Testament more often ascribes wealth accumulation to exploitation and predatory practices than to individual hard work), the Jubilee imperative testifies to the divine economy as one of abundance rather than scarcity, of communal sufficiency rather than individual acquisition.

Just as Christians have labored mightily to evade the unambiguous and uncomfortable imperatives of the Sermon on the Mount, so too did the Israelites often seek to avoid the radical Sabbath and Jubilee practices commanded by Yahweh. As Myers notes (see also Ellul, 1980):

> The historical narratives in the Hebrew Bible indicate that as the tribal confederacy was eclipsed by centralized political power under the Davidic dynasty, economic stratification followed inextricably. Indeed, the prophet Samuel warned that a monarchy would be linked intrinsically to an economy geared to the elite through ruthless policies of surplus-extraction and militarism (1 Sam. 8:11–18).

Israel's prophetic tradition preserved Sabbath and Jubilee economics as a living force by criticizing the nation's leaders for abandoning the poor and centralizing wealth in the hands of a few. The promise of Jubilee eventually came to be part of eschatological hope in postexilic Judaism—the coming of the kingdom would mean this-worldly changes in the lot of the poor by vigorous practice of Jubilee economics, including the forgiveness of sins and debts (Wright, 1996; Myers, 1998). When Jesus turns to Isaiah 61:1–2 to announce the beginning of his public ministry, he proclaims the start of "the year of the Lord's favor"—a Jubilee year, with revolutionary import in his day that provoked the powerful against him.

So, to look to the Sermon on the Mount as a starting point for an economics for discipleship, one immediately begins with dangerous materials. Jesus' intensified appropriation of Israel's economic law runs throughout the Sermon, providing his disciples and interested onlookers with insights into the sort of practices and relations needed to be a follower of Jesus. Whether he talks about forgiving sins and debts, or healing the sick, or proclaiming the arrival of the kingdom, Jesus is announcing that Israel's economic hopes are being fulfilled in the arrival of the kingdom, which is being modeled in the practices of his followers.

"Give to anyone who asks you" (Matt. 5:42 NJB).

Jesus calls upon his disciples to practice an economics of abundance—to imitate the profligate generosity of God, who gives generously to all humanity regardless of merit. The presumption that abundance rather than scarcity forms the basis of creation distinguishes discipleship economics from all secular schools of economics, in which scarcity is the foundational assumption (D. Stephen Long, 1999). Learning how to follow Jesus includes economic practices that are illogical, shortsighted, and foolish in the world's eyes; what kind of organization gives to everyone who asks? What kind of security can one enjoy if he or she follows Jesus' directive that "if anyone wants to borrow, do not turn away" (NJB)?

In fact, a redirection of security is primary in Jesus' economic practice. His disciples are instructed to pray for *daily* bread—not unlimited bread, not a month's worth, not a storage facility for surplus bread but *daily* bread—trusting that God will provide for God's people just as Yahweh provided for Israel in the desert. In return for God's daily fidelity and generosity, disciples are instructed to pray for (and themselves grant) debt forgiveness—inaugurating Jubilee practices among themselves in the here and now, an unmistakable light for the world (5:15) and sign that in fact "Your Kingdom [has] come," because Yahweh's will is now being done on earth as presumably it always has been done in heaven (6:10).

The sort of economic practices needed to be a follower of Jesus are demanding and not likely to be popular choices (7:13–14). Most people will continue to place their trust in their possessions, will look to family and wealth for protection against scarcity instead of to Jesus and His followers. That kind of strategy may work well enough for some purposes, but it is decidedly inadequate for Jesus' purposes—it does not announce the inbreaking of the kingdom, it cannot stand as a beacon inviting others into God's new experiment, and it cannot be good news to the poor.

The Lillies of the Field

The key to the Sermon's contribution to an economics of discipleship may lie in 6:25–34 (NJB):

That is why I am telling you not to worry about your life and what you are to eat, nor about your body and what you are to wear. Surely life is more than food, and the body more than clothing! Look at the birds in the sky. They do not sow or reap or gather into barns; yet your heavenly Father feeds them. Are you not worth much more than they are? Can any of you, however much you worry, add one single cubit to your span of life? And why worry about clothing? Think of the flowers ["lillies," in the older translations] growing in the fields; they never have to work or spin; yet I assure you that not even Solomon in all his royal robes was clothed like one of these. Now if that is how God clothes the wild flowers growing in the field which are there today and thrown into the furnace tomorrow, will he not much more look after you, you who have so little faith? So do not worry; do not say, "What are we to eat? What are we to drink? What are we to wear?" It is the gentiles who set their hearts on all these things. Your heavenly Father knows you need them all. Set your hearts on his kingdom first, and on God's saving justice, and all these other things will be given you as well. So do not worry about tomorrow; tomorrow will take care of itself. Each day has enough trouble of its own.

Jesus makes outrageous promises here, offering plenitude and freedom from the anxiety scarcity produces to those who seek and live in the kingdom and in the justice it brings. Yet we live in a world in which billions go hungry, in which millions of children die too soon while the wealthy gorge themselves. What has happened to these outrageous promises? Does God not keep God's word?

We suggest the promises remain valid, that God stands ready to deliver as promised. Thus far, however, these promises have been thwarted by our unwillingness to live as if "thy Kingdom came"—we block the promises by still being slaves to money (6:24). Because we have not trusted in God's abundance, and because we have not risked our security by trusting the new brothers and sisters given to us by God, the outrageous promises of God are choked off, and in fact burn like cruel, impossible dreams—when we have frustrated the preconditions for their fulfillment from the outset.

What might it mean to live as slaves to money, as persons who put their faith in treasures stored on earth (6:19–21, 24)? It means to live as all of us do—as enslaved to an economy in bondage to scarcity, aggressive acquisition, and sharp dealings with others. We know what life is like in this kind of bondage—it is the same kind of bondage that typified the "fleshpots" of Israel's material security in Egypt (Exod. 16:2–3)—and as discussed elsewhere in this book, we know that such bondage cannot form people into true followers of Jesus.

A necessary corollary to the economy of abundance Jesus promises is a community that knows how to pray effectively:

> Ask, and it will be given to you; search, and you will find; knock, and the door will be opened to you. Everyone who asks receives; everyone who searches finds; everyone who knocks will have the door opened. Is there anyone among you who would hand his son a stone when he asked for bread? Or would hand him a snake when he asked for a fish? If you, then, evil as you are, know how to give your children what is good, how much more will your Father in heaven give good things to those who ask him! (Matt. 7:7–11 NJB)

Not only does Jesus make promises of abundance, he legitimates an economic ethic of *demand*—persons striving to live as if the kingdom has already begun need only to ask for what they need, and God will provide. Since the church has long been recognized as "God's hands" on earth, doing for the world as God intends, the community that prays and the community that responds to prayer is one and the same—the people whose life is lived in mission, who have found freedom from scarcity by trusting in God's abundance as mediated by and through the gathered people of God.

As if aware that such outrageous promises would attract charlatans and entrepreneurs, Jesus counsels his followers about false prophets (7:15–20). Since the test is "by their fruits," those whose counsel makes available the bounty of God through the life of discipleship can be trusted. Similarly, false prophets in our day might be those who retard this abundance and daily trust in God, those who counsel the ways of transnational firms rather than the new manna-fed Israel, who breed competition and self-promotion within the body of Christ. Such an ethic, and the prophets who bring it, will assure that the kingdom will never be recognized in our world, and in fact will try to prevent its coming at all.

From the Sermon to the *Ekklesia*

Two considerations need to be noted here: the discipleship ethic described by the Sermon is a communal phenomenon rather than one aimed at isolated individuals, and the Sermon presupposes lives formed by the gospel and Christian practices. In taking the Sermon as a "magna carta" of gospel morality, we are making claims about what the church should do and be—a very different matter than designing a polity or economy for communities that do not accept the lordship of Christ. The point is not to design a more "moral" polity or economy for everyone else—another version of the Constantinian temptation, a false obligation laid upon the church—but to demonstrate to everyone else what lives dedicated to the kingdom of God might look like in our world. People "called out" into the *ekklesia* by God will never live the Sermon's vision perfectly, and certainly not on their own, but with God's help they might move in a direction noticeably different from others. They might be better examples of God's prototype for human sociability, built on mutuality and forgiveness rather than coercion and division.

Before the mainstream of Christianity lost its desire to live as a polity and *oikos* tied to the Kingdom, it experimented with various ways of living the Sermon's political economy. The shared property of the Jerusalem church (Acts 2–4) and Paul's program of ecclesial economic solidarity were just two among many examples. Even after the compromises that substituted Christendom for the kingdom of God, numerous reformers and innovators reclaimed or inaugurated economic practices better able to "make disciples" in their time and place.

But what about our time? What kind of economic practices might be better suited to the task of making Christians than the practices and ideologies of contemporary capitalism? Can we do better than Christianity Incorporated?

We might begin by interrogating some existing church practices for residues, clues, or harbingers of economic practices more attuned to the political economy of the Sermon than of Wall Street. Within these practices reside some resources capable of resisting Christianity Incorporated and building some requisites for an economics of discipleship.

The Economic Structure of the Soup Line

Basic Christian charity—providing food, clothing, shelter, and the like—has been a defining aspect of church practice since the movement's beginning. A closer look at one sort of charitable practice—the church-run soup kitchen—provides evidence of the Sermon's economic vision still alive in our world of accommodated Christianity. By examining the economic structure of the soup line, we can get hints of what a discipleship-centered economy might include.

Consider the labor structure of a church soup line. Whether one is a surgeon or a fast food employee in the secular world, one is just a "worker" in the soup kitchen. Surgeons don't get easier or more interesting jobs than anyone else, investment bankers don't get to give the orders to the secretaries, and people whose education and wealth entitle them to status in the secular world find those without purchase when making meals for the poor. The soup kitchen's labor structure, in other words, does two important things: it reverses secular hierarchies of influence and privilege, and it de-differentiates the labor process—no specialization, no highly developed division of labor that gives some people interesting and creative work while leaving dangerous or drudge work to others. Both of those features of soup kitchen labor are relevant to an economics of discipleship—if the hierarchies of wealth, race, and merit that stratify the secular world are reproduced in doing the Lord's work, then the illuminative quality of the church as a new community reflective of the kingdom is lost. Similarly, if the church accepts uncritically the creation of job complexes that give interesting and creative work tasks to some while forcing others into mindless, stultifying, and degrading labor, it perpetuates the negative formative effects of much contemporary work and obscures the freedom that comes from following Christ and Christ's example in our world.

Consider also the distributive policies of a church soup kitchen. Most reflect the Sermon's directive to "Give to all who ask." Healthy-looking people are not refused food, nor are the overweight or better dressed. Church soup kitchens do not employ means tests or co-pay requirements. They practice the sort of "manna economy" built into the Hebrew economic ethic—they do not refuse to feed hungry people today in order to hoard food for tomorrow. So long as there are people waiting to eat, and so long as there is food to provide them, the soup kitchen serves without cold calculations about tomorrow. The degree of trust involved—that if today's food is exhausted, somehow God will provide food for the next time—becomes a lived part of the process instead of an unrealistic abstraction.

But it is when examining the provisioning of the church soup kitchen that the opportunities and pitfalls attendant to an economics of discipleship become most apparent. While the soup kitchen provides an important sort of social alchemy—taking a commodified basic need like food and transmuting it into a decommodified resource available for the asking—provisioning the soup kitchen stands as an important point of contact between the *ekklesia* and the capitalist world.

The first thing to notice is that most church soup kitchens are relentlessly opportunistic in their approach to provisions. They seek out money, donations, contributions, and leftovers from a variety of sources, sometimes from sources that are opposed to the social vision of the churches. Soup kitchens survive on the margins of the capitalist machine, but can they do so without being shaped by that machinery? Can one beg for government surplus and corporate largesse while maintaining a social theology still capable of an anticapitalist posture? Too close of an identification of the soup kitchen with powerful benefactors turns the work into a puppet of the powerful, a show pony for state and corporate public relations. Such problems have always been attached to the sort of mendicancy that soup kitchens (and other religious works that depend upon begging for their survival) represent.

Being an opportunist means employing the sort of "weapons of the weak" studied by James Scott (1985) and others. It involves a willingness to engage in a certain degree of dissembling, providing a frontstage posture that is less offensive to the powerful while displaying one's more authentic dispositions in backstage venues, swallowing one's pride and militance in order to meet the needs of the poor and vulnerable. Such approaches must stay strictly in the realm of tactics (rather than one's primary strategy), however; being able to refuse patronage that comes with too high a price is essential if one is to place trust in a God that will provide a better deal somehow. It represents a difficult balancing act that requires prudential judgment and Christian wisdom and maturity.

One way out of some of these provisioning dilemmas has been explored by the Catholic Worker movement and its predecessors in religious life, for whom soup kitchens have been tied to productive agricultural labor. Peter Maurin's idea of "agronomic universities" tied to urban houses of hospitality was intended to provide food for the hungry, work and skills development for the unemployed, and employment structures that reduced the status and privilege gaps between mental and manual labor. While many of the Catholic Worker's experiments in farming failed due to insufficient planning and serious undercapitalization, they provide examples relevant to the larger church-as-*oikos* as one way to build economic linkages—"backward" into the supply and development of raw materials and inputs, and "forward" into distribution. What possibilities might emerge were established churches, dioceses, and denominations to begin their own experiments with production of essential goods and services?

Were the churches to explore creating their own backward linkages, from their soup kitchens to the production of the food they use, they would likely encounter the following:

—A gradual restoration of skills lost from the deskilling of labor by certain forms of technological organization, from the push of people from rural lifestyles into urban and suburban ones; and opportunities for blended job complexes that involve work of

many different types (de-differentiation of employment structures);

—A long-term means of providing employment to persons now
unemployed or underemployed. Unlike make-work programs or
those tied to corporate imperatives, this sort of initiative would
provide useful work tied to the public expression of the ecclesial
identity of the church and its members. People could do important and meaningful work directly tied to the mission of the
church—an experience quite different from the meaningless or
irrelevant work many people are forced to perform;

—Eventually a reduced reliance on commodified sources of
food and other essentials for church programs, and hence reduced
reliance on corporate donors and patrons;

—A practical, hands-on means for all churches (rich and poor,
in various settings) to make the much-discussed but under-
practiced "option for the poor." As workers, as consumers, as directors, and as partners, poor people inside and outside the church
would be major participants and beneficiaries of such efforts.

What such initiatives bring to the fore, in addition, is the conflict between economic mobility (fueled especially by market
forces) and geographic proximity. Capitalism, whatever else it
does, stands for the triumph of speed over place—that is, the rapid
turnover and adjustments that markets demand work against all
but trivialized notions of settled communities that endure over
time in a particular location. The tyranny of capital flight, which
impoverishes some areas while forcing others to bribe businesses
to invest in their communities, destroys the kind of geographical
proximity that churches need if they are to exist as polities and
economies in service to the kingdom rather than to the existing
powers. Increased migration, the dividing of families and separa-
tion of people from neighborhoods, relatives, and fellow church
members—these flow from capital mobility and state policies that
shape and are shaped by that mobility. These sort of dynamics
produce impermanent, superficial ecclesial relations. The kind of
trust and intimacy necessary for churches to live out more fully
their mission is thwarted by the reality of job turnover, family
relocations, and other individualized means of coping with the

intrinsic instability of capitalism. Churches then might as well be standardized filling stations that "meet customers' needs," since they are unlikely to be anything more than that. The farther apart church members live, and the more their unity is denied by the mobility and transience required by market processes, the less able the church is to do anything else.

A church that takes itself and its own economics seriously will work to reemphasize place, will structure economic practices that make it easier for churches to stay together longer, and will encourage economic practices that allow congregants to enter one another's lives more deeply and completely. But what sort of structures and practices could churches adopt to strengthen the power of place, to make ecclesial goods and services production a possibility that didn't merely imitate the worst aspects of for-profit firms? While the diverse circumstances of churches militates against a one-size-fits-all approach, one might consider a range of integrated options that include:

—Church-based credit unions dedicated to encouraging church members to live close to one another—as neighbors, in other words;

—New experiments in labor sharing. One possibility would be for churches to adopt variations on "labor currency" practices used in some secular communities, in which people exchange their labor time and skills for those of other members of the church. Such barter not only frees up church members' time and money, it also stands as another ecclesial protest against capitalist labor differentiation and privilege, inasmuch as an hour of a doctor's time is not treated as being worth three hundred hours of a fellow Christian cleaning woman's time. Another experiment in labor sharing would be a "labor tithe" to accompany the (unevenly utilized) practice of a money tithe: instead of (or in addition) to cash pledges proportionate to one's income, churches could also collect pledges of time from members. These labor tithes could be used intra-ecclesially or extra-ecclesially on projects tied to the social ministry of the church. These sorts of experiments go beyond traditional volunteerism, which involves a minuscule proportion of congregants in many denominations (for Catholic figures, see

Castelli and Gremillion, 1987), both because they are expectations laid upon all church members as they are able, and because they are economically significant in what they make it possible to do (and avoid).

—Church-based consumers' cooperatives, workshops, and appliance centers, important both for work and household needs. Church members can access tools and training—from carpentry to computers—without every member of the church having to absorb such expenses individually (and without having to earn the extra cash incomes necessary to acquire and support them). Middle-class and working-class households alike can drastically lower their household expenses by being freed from the need for each to purchase and maintain their own clothes washers and dryers, snowblowers, saws, drills, trucks, computers, specialized gardening and cooking equipment, and more. Such efforts that reduce the need for increased cash incomes could free up congregants' time and resources, hopefully for more kingdom-centered efforts (the works of mercy, evangelization, social witness, etc.).

If the church begins to enter into experiments with economic production, common consumption, and labor allocation/organization, it can offer some hope of ransoming some of its members from unemployment, work in immoral occupations (drug dealing, weapons industries, advertising, etc.), or work under exploitative or inhumane conditions. Church-centered economic experiments will not work perfectly, of course, and the churches will still find themselves engaged with capitalist practices at the same time—but they might provide some hint of possibilities and new directions as yet unexplored.

Learning From Existing Efforts

Some churches and church-related agencies have been aware of the need for church-centered economic experiments for some time. Other church leaders, more interested in boosting numbers at any cost or constructing their own economic fiefdoms, have launched enterprises in which radical discipleship has been an obstacle rather than an objective.

Examples of church-based economic experiments worth further scrutiny include some from rather improbable places. We have been among those harboring serious reservations about the so-called megachurch phenomenon, but we cannot deny that Willow Creek Community Church has launched a few interesting economic initiatives. While it remains unclear whether these types of ventures can serve churches with a clearer sense of distinctiveness from dominant American ideologies remains to be seen, Willow Creek ventures like the following deserve greater church exploration:

—The church established a ministry among its members called Christian Auto Repairmen Serving (CARS), which provided three hundred free auto repairs and fixed one hundred and twenty cars later given to needy church families;

—The church also created a group of thirty hairdressers that provide their services free to abused and battered women, unwed pregnant women, the homeless, and clients of the church's food pantry;

—Willow Creek also has four self-sustaining ministries. One of them, a catering service named Harvest, sold 480,000 meals to church attendees and conference participants in 1999, enabling it to cover its annual budget of $2.4 million while utilizing the efforts of seven hundred church volunteers (see Gillmor, 2000).

Far from Willow Creek's niche in the contemporary ecclesial landscape are thousands of African-American churches for which economic innovation has long been a necessity rather than an option. Even more so than in white middle-class churches, assessing the transformative potential of African-American church-based economic practices is a difficult matter. A wide array of economic practices past and present inform African-American church history, a diversity that demands attention as much as whatever consistencies one can discern. From antigovernmental self-help programs to federally funded corporate entrepreneurs, from co-operatives to real estate speculation—the range of church-based ventures emerging from the black church continues to be broad.

But just as the experiments themselves reflect a diversity of approaches, so too there is no consensus among African-American churches on how best to relate to political and economic processes in which they are often neglected or weak participants. Should the churches embrace capitalist values and practices? Should they enhance the New Deal/Great Society vision of public-private partnerships as manifested, for example, in community development corporations? Or should they reject and resist capitalism and its practices in favor of community- and church-based co-operatives, as described by Marcus Garvey and later W. E. B. DuBois (for an important overview, see Shipp, 1996)?

It is difficult to determine in advance what programs of a particular church are or are not consistent with an economics of discipleship—and it is especially problematic for middle-class white Christians to pass judgment on the choices made by African-American churches. One starting point in the discussion, however, might be for churches of all varieties to work toward identifying approaches that provide resources and alternatives to capitalism and its effects broadly construed (which frequently work to the detriment of Christian mission and community, as argued throughout this book and elsewhere).

In other words, economic production, job creation, or any other aspect of economic activity might be insufficient in itself. Rather, consideration must expand to include attention to how production, employment, or other aspects affect Christian formation and socialization, whether they tend to unify or fragment the body of Christ, and whether the activities do or do not advance ecclesial mission and service. These sorts of considerations would militate against some sort of church-based economic ventures (those that seek merely to create a class of Christian capitalists, business owners, or entrepreneurs that claim to follow a thin gloss of "biblical principles" in their management styles).

Economic practices proffered as Christian business that in fact inhibit rather than advance ecclesial and gospel-based notions of discipleship are all too easily found. They shine through in the work of people who equate the church with "a new business start-up, a small-cap, high-risk aggressive growth venture" (Robert A. Chestnut, quoted in Paulsell, 2000, p. 1189). The progeny of Bruce Barton also stand at cross purposes to what we advocate. The urge to harmonize Christianity, free enterprise, and a strong America continues the effacement of ecclesial identity and the radical kingdom in favor of chaplaincy to capitalism and the state (e.g., Gahr, 1997, p. 54).

Similarly, firms that trumpet their "Christian" management principles but subvert unionization among their employees (e.g., Servicemaster, some Catholic hospital corporations) or support pro-capitalist advocacy groups and parties (e.g., Interstate Batteries, Amway) do not exemplify what we intend (Gahr, 1997, pp. 54–56; also McGraw, 1995, pp. 53–54). Even the notion of intra-ecclesial economic solidarity—patronizing the firms of one's fellow Christians over those without ties to the church or its mission (a notion we think deserves further exploration, despite the dubious legacy of some past experiments with it)—can be twisted toward objectives still deeply tied to Constantinian models of church power and statecraft (for example, Pat Robertson's advocacy of "buy Christian" as another way to fund conservative political organizations; McGraw, 1995, p. 59).

Similarly, we cannot see how church development as a "school for disciples," in which self-sacrifice in the service of the exploited and marginalized, is advanced by programs like that of the Catholic Archdiocese of Rio de Janeiro. Frustrated by the inability of traditional forms of Catholic fundraising to provide resources for charitable work, the archdiocese plans a stock issue that sells shares in the Church's charitable organization to corporate investors. As described by a corporate advisor to the plan, this stock offering allows corporate "fund managers to buy into the good name of the Church by putting their money into its social programmes." The plan further removes the economics of the works of mercy from the lives of most Christians since, as the advisor notes, "Only serious financial people will be able to buy the stock because the Church needs large sums of money to continue its work, not well-meaning smaller donations." Shareholders will be allowed to choose which social programs they will support, from orphanages to HIV care initiatives (Veash, 2000).

While stock exchange official Carlos Alberto Reis may be enthralled about the plan because "this launch is one way of redeeming [investors]," from here it looks like yet another capitulation of the church to the logic of capitalism. Whether contemplating the fate of ministries that fail to create an investors' "buzz," or the reluctance of church leaders to espouse positions that might prompt "capital flight" from its work, the prospects of ending up with a church that worships God rather than mammon (and whose works of mercy are owned by corporate investors in a church in which the Sermon on the Mount belongs in the prospectus and nowhere else) seem progressively dimmed. At a minimum, it is a long way from the Widow's Mite (Luke 21:1–4).

If these sorts of practices do not seem helpful in moving toward an economics of discipleship, are there other examples that point toward that goal? If we return to the experiences of some African-American churches, at least some economic initiatives emerged from a desire to resist the effects of capitalism and commodification; some of these noncapitalist initiatives in the black church drew inspiration from co-operative enterprises started under Catholic auspices in Spain early in the twentieth century—namely, in the Basque region called Mondragon (Shipp, 1996).

The Mondragon system of producer and consumer co-operatives has generated much literature (more than seventy books and sixty major articles, according to Whyte, 1999), and is not without its problems and limitations (Kasmir, 1996). But compared to the practices of "Christian capitalism" just described, Mondragon-style efforts do leave more room to develop the ecclesial character of an economics of discipleship. While even the largest co-ops remain within the intricacies of the global market, their stress on solidarity within and among co-operatives, member participation, and nonmarket values distinguish them from the organizational forms that dominate contemporary capitalism (for an overview, see Hill, 2000). Even given the compromises forced upon them by capitalist pressures (how damning those compromises have been continues to be in dispute), Mondragon-style co-ops still attempt to institutionalize practices that privilege worker participation and decision making of a degree and kind beyond that obtained in most employee stock-ownership programs (ESOPs), portfolio stock ownership, and Japanese-style labor processes. These latter forms, variously aimed at boosting labor productivity, buying labor peace, or some other set of goals, do not (or no longer, in the case of ESOPs) see themselves as socializing their participants in economic practices capable of contesting the ideologies and imperatives of global capitalism.

Churches of many varieties have experimented with producer co-ops, consumer co-ops, and co-operative marketing and distribution efforts—indeed, the leadership of churches is often considered a crucial variable in many co-operatives' efforts, given churches' demonstrated abilities to call forth short-term sacrifices for the communal good and to limit so-called "free rider" problems. Granted that church-related co-ops have varied dramatically historically—some indistinguishable from capitalist firms in essential matters, others laboring as midwives of social revolution and targeted for death by state and economic elites, with others somewhere in between—more research and experimentation are needed to assess how co-ops aid, inhibit, or do not influence important processes of ecclesial formation, mission, and social engagement. While Mondragon itself may no longer have the ability to resist the corrosive effects—ideological and operational—of capitalism, it may yet inspire new experiments in which the *ekklesia* is the primary focus instead of one ally in a larger (ethnic and national) vision.

For persons more deeply schooled by Adam Smith than the Sermon on the Mount, the notion of the "church as *oikos*" doubtless sounds absurd and irresponsible. Another consequence of centuries of accommodated Christianity is a loss of collective imagination and creativity—having grown used to seeing the church as a salve or counsel to a more fundamental set of realities and practices, it becomes difficult to imagine the body of Christ as being capable of practices that more clearly reflect the outrageous promises and priorities of Jesus and God's kingdom. This poverty of imagination and experimentation—which has produced too few "useful" examples of church practices we advocate—then itself becomes "proof" that no other future for the church is possible other than the chaplain's role it has performed so thoroughly.

This self-fulfilling counsel to minimal Christianity becomes yet another season of despair to be blasted away by the good news of

the kingdom, in which God's promises become more fully realized to and through churches that dare to believe, trust, and act
in the Spirit of divine extravagance. May it be so sooner rather
than later.

Works Cited

Ackers, Peter, & Preston, Diane. (1997). Born Again? The ethics and efficacy of the conversion experience in contemporary management development. *Journal of Management Studies* 32(5).

American Demographics. (1997). Advertising joins the journey of the soul. June.

Austin, Nancy. (1995). Does spirituality at work work? *Working Women* 20(3).

Barton, Bruce. (1925). *The Man Nobody Knows.* Indianapolis: Bobbs-Merrill.

Blackburn, Tom. (1995). Virtue in America is about getting ahead. *National Catholic Reporter,* November 3.

Boshoff, Allison. (1998). Advertisers are told to curb jokes on religion. *Daily Telegraph,* August 12.

Brandt, Ellen. (1996). Corporate pioneers explore spirituality, peace. *HR Magazine,* April.

Breuer, Nancy. (1997). When workers seek pastoral advice—how will you answer them? *Workforce,* April.

Brown, Tom. (1995). Jesus CEO. *Industry Week,* March 6.

Bryce, Robert. (1999). The dying giant. *Salon,* September 29.

———. (1996). Merchant of Death. *Texas Monthly,* June.

Budde, Michael. (1997). *The (Magic) Kingdom of God: Christianity and Global Culture Industries.* Boulder, Colo.: Westview.

Cahill, Lisa Sowle. (1994). *Love Your Enemies: Discipleship, Pacifism, and Just War Theory.* Minneapolis: Fortress.

California Public Interest Research Group (Calpirg). (1998) *Can You Afford to Die? A Calpirg Report on the Prices, Practices, and Oversight of the Funeral Industry.*

Castelli, Jim, & Gremillion, Joseph. (1987). *The Emerging Parish: The Notre Dame Study of Catholic Life.* New York: Harper and Row.

Charry, Tamar. (1997). Where's the latest trend? At the intersection of Madison Avenue and the paths of righteousness. *New York Times,* May 6.

Christian Century. (1996). Europeans seek the grave's anonymity. May 15.

Clapp, Rodney. (1993). *Families at the Crossroads.* Downers Grove, Ill.: InterVarsity Press.

Cohen, Andy. (1997). The Lowe down. *Sales and Marketing Management* 149:8.

Combe, Victoria. (1999). Church plans market research to gauge views of "customers." *Daily Telegraph,* February 18.

———. (1997). Church puts its faith in TV advertisement. *Daily Telegraph,* March 20.

Cooper, Cary. (1999). The changing psychological contract at work. *European Business Journal,* 11:3.

Cormode, D. Scott. (1998). Does institutional isomorphism imply secularization? In N. J. Demerath III, Hall, Peter Dobkin, Schmitt, Terry, & Williams, Rhys H. (Eds.), *Sacred Companies.* London: Oxford University Press.

Daily Telegraph. (1999). Worship in the fast lane. January 4.

Daniels, James. (1997). The command master religious plan: A cost model for chaplaincy activities in the United States Army. *Armed Forces Comptroller.* Winter.

Davis, Kristin. (1997). Paying for the funeral. *Kiplinger's Personal Finance Magazine,* May.

Demerath, N. J. III, Hall, Peter Dobkin, Schmitt, Terry, & Williams, Rhys H. (Eds.) (1997). *Sacred Companies.* London: Oxford University Press.

D'Emilio, Frances. (1999). Vatican embraces corporate sponso *Associated Press,* September 30.

Denman, Ann McKistry. (1992). C.C.D.: "Central City Dum *America,* October 3.

Department of Consumer Affairs, city of New York. (1999). *Report on Funeral Industry*. February 11.

Dietrich, Jeff. (1996). Death is the most natural thing in the world. *National Catholic Reporter,* July 26.

DiMaggio, Paul, & Powell, Walter. (1991). The iron cage revisited: Institutional isomorphism and collective rationality. In Powell, Walter W., & DiMaggio, Paul J., (Eds.), *The New Institutionalism in Organizational Analysis*. Chicago: University of Chicago Press.

Downey, William. (1998). Secular rites. *Christian Century,* April 8.

Dumais, Marcel. (1998). The Sermon on the Mount: An unattainable way of life? *Chicago Studies,* 37:3.

Dumestre, Marcel. (1993). Toward effective adult religious education. *Origins,* May 27.

Ekstrom, Reynolds R. (1992). Consumerism and youth. In Ekstrom, Reynolds R. (Ed.), *Media and Culture*. New Rochelle, N.Y.: Don Bosco/Multimedia Press.

Ellul, Jacques. (1980). Christianity and Anarchism. *Katallegete.*

Fagan, Patrick F. (1996). Why religion matters: The impact of religious practice on social stability. Washington, D.C.: The Heritage Foundation.

FAMSA (Funeral and Mortuary Societies of America). (1999). Comments on the Federal Trade Commission Review of the Funeral Rule. Available at www.funerals.org/famsa.htm.

Fields, Robin. (1999). Archdiocese's mortuary deal raises eyebrows. *Los Angeles Times,* November 13.

Firat, A. Fuat. (1991). The consumer in postmodernity. *Advances in Consumer Research.* 18.

Fisher, Daniel. (1999). Grave dancer. *Forbes,* June 14.

Flecker-Feltz, Cheryl. (1993). Chaplains become big business. *National Catholic Reporter.* August 13.

Friedman, Thomas. (1999). A manifesto for the fast world. *New York Times Sunday Magazine,* March 28; quoted in T. Howland Sanks, 1999, Globalization and the church's social mission. *Theological Studies.* 60.

Gahr, Evan. (1997). Spirited Enterprise. *The American Enterprise,* July/August.

Gallup, George Jr., & Castelli, Jim. (1987). *The American Catholic People*. Garden City, N.Y.: Doubleday.

Gandy, Oscar. (1993). *The Panoptic Sort: A Political Economy of Personal Information.* Boulder, Colo.: Westview Press.

Gibeau, Dawn. (1994). Catholic education groups collaborate on what to teach and in what manner. *National Catholic Reporter,* July 29.

Gillmor, Verla. (2000). Community is our middle name. *Christianity Today.* November 13.

Glendhill, Ruth. (1999). Churches turn to Mammon for the millennium. *Times of London,* September 16.

Goldman, Ari. (1994). The marketing of the Pope. *New York Times,* August 27.

Goodstein, Laurie. (2000). Archbishop-elect is a man who takes charge. *New York Times,* May 12.

Greeley, Andrew. (1997). The other civic America: religion and social capital. *American Prospect,* May/June.

Grossman, David. (1995). *On Killing.* New York: Back Bay/Little, Brown and Company.

Harrington, Daniel. (1998). The Sermon on the Mount: What is it? *The Bible Today,* September.

Harris, Marlyn. (1997). The final payment. *Monday,* September.

Harvey, David. (1989). *The Condition of Postmodernity.* Oxford: Blackwell.

Hauerwas, Stanley. (1995). *In Good Company: The Church as Polis.* Notre Dame, Ind.: University of Notre Dame Press.

Hays, Richard. (1996). *The Moral Vision of the New Testament.* New York: HarperCollins.

Heilke, Thomas. (1997). Locating a moral/political economy: lessons from sixteenth-century Anabaptism. *Polity.* 30:2.

Herman, Edward, and Noam Chomsky. (1988). *Manufacturing Consent.* New York: Pantheon.

Hill, Roderick. (2000). The case of the mission organizations: co-operatives and the textbooks. *Journal of Economic Education,* Summer.

Horn, Miriam. (1998). The deathcare business. *U.S. News and World Report,* March 23.

Jacobson, Michael, and Laurie Ann Mazur. (1995). *Marketing Madness.* Boulder, Colo.: Westview.

Jameson, Frederic. (1991). *Postmodernism: Or the Cultural Logic of Late Capitalism*. Durham, N.C.: Duke University Press.

Janofsky, Michael. (1993). In defense of the Pope's brand name. *New York Times*, June 14.

Jones, Laurie Beth. (1995). *Jesus CEO: Using Ancient Wisdom for Visionary Leadership*. New York: Hyperion Press.

Jordan, Pat. (1997). In Deepak we trust. *Sales and Marketing Management*. 149:8.

Kamakure, Wagner, & Novak, Thomas. (1992). Value-system segmentation: Exploring the meaning of LOV. *Journal of Consumer Research*. No. 19.

Kasmir, Sharya. (1996). *The Myth of Mondragon: Cooperatives, Politics and Working-Class Life in a Basque Town*. Albany, N.Y.: SUNY Press.

Kingsnorth, Paul. (1999). A very happy birthday for NAFTA. *The Ecologist*, January–February.

Klare, Michael, & Kornbluh, Peter (Eds.). (1987). *Low Intensity Conflict*. New York: Pantheon.

Krueger, Jill. (1998). Big death braces for a big battle in Tallahassee. *Orlando Business Journal*, November 27.

Laabs, Jennifer. (1995). Balancing spirituality and work. *Personnel Journal*, September.

Larson, Erik. (1996). Fight to the death. *Time*, December 9.

Leigh, Pamela. (1997). The new spirit at work. *Training and Development*, March.

Leonard, Bill. (2000). Employees feel good about job security. *HR Magazine*, March.

Leiss, William, Kline, Stephen, & Jhally, Sut. (1990). *Social Communication in Advertising*, 2d ed. New York: Routledge.

Libbon, Robert. (1999). Has anyone done any projections on how the baby boomers may increase the demand for gravestones? *American Demographics*. 21:1.

Linder, Robert. (1996). Universal pastor: President Bill Clinton's civil religion. *Journal of Church and State*, Autumn.

Locke, John. *Second Treatise on Government*. (1690). (1980). Indianapolis, Ind.: Hackett Publishing.

Loewen Group. (1999). Annual Report.

Long, Cynthia. (1997). Attention all worshippers: Public relations activities of the churches. *Insight on the News,* March 31.

Long, D. Stephen. (1999). *Divine Economy.* New York: Routledge.

Long, Thomas G. (1999). Why Jessica Mitford was wrong. *Theology Today.* 55:4.

Longworth, R. C. (1998). The start of the American Century. *Chicago Tribune,* April 12.

Management Services. (2000). IPD research shatters myth of the dissatisfied and insecure British worker. January.

Marketing. (1997). The church needs a marketing miracle. April 17.

Marketing News. (1992). Mythologies can help build brands. February 17.

Marriott, Robin. (1986). Ads require sensitivity to Arab culture. *Marketing News,* April 25.

Mattelart, Armand. (1991). *Advertising International.* New York: Routledge.

McChesney, Robert. (1998). The political economy of global media. *Media Development,* No. 4.

McGraw, Dan. (1995). The Christian capitalists. *U.S. News and World Report,* March 13.

McIllroy, A. J., & Combe, Victoria. (1997). Carey warns against creating barriers to baptism. *Daily Telegraph,* April 14.

Micklethwait, John, & Woodridge, Adrian. (1996). *The Witch Doctors.* New York: Times Business Publishers.

Mongovern, Anne Marie. (1992). Catechesis in the 90s: Present state and future challenges. *Chicago Studies.* 31:2.

Morgan, Edward S. (1965). *Puritan Political Ideas.* Indianapolis, Ind.: Bobbs-Merrill.

Murray-Brown, Jeremy. (1991). Video ergo sum. In *Video Icons and Values,* Olson, A., Parr, C., & Parr, D. Albany, N.Y.: SUNY Press.

Myers, Ched. (1998). Jesus' new economy of grace/God speed the year of Jubilee. *Sojourners.* May–June and July–August.

Neal, Judith. (1997). Spirituality in management education: A guide to resources. *Journal of Management Education,* February.

Neck, Christopher, & Milliman, John. (1994). Thought self-leadership: Finding spiritual fulfillment in organizational life. *Journal of Management Psychology.* 96.

Neuhaus, Richard John. (1997). The liberalism of John Paul II. *First Things.* May.

————. (1992). *Doing Well and Doing Good.* New York: Doubleday.

Newman, Judith. (1997). At your disposal. *Harpers,* November.

Newsnet 5 (Cleveland). (1998). Roman Catholic Church unfair? *Associated Press,* August 4.

Nolan, James L. (1996). Affirming the relevance of religious faith to business practices: An address to the Fourth International Forum, International Association of Jesuit Business Schools, Los Angeles. July 29. Available at www.georgetown.edu/centers/woodstock/wbc/wbc-aff.htm.

Novak, Michael. (1999). How Christianity created capitalism. *Wall Street Journal,* December 23.

————. (1993). *The Catholic Ethic and the Spirit of Capitalism.* New York: Free Press.

————. (1989). *Free Persons and the Common Good.* Lanham, Md.: Madison Books.

————. (1982). *The Spirit of Democratic Capitalism.* New York: Simon and Schuster.

Orsi, Michael P. (1994). Catechesis in the third millennium. *Religious Education.* 89:3.

Paulsell, Stephanie. (2000). Gospel ventures. *Christian Century,* November 15.

Peikoff, Leonard. (1997). Has Christmas become too commercial? No way. *Las Vegas Review Journal,* December 21.

Piirto, Rebecca. (1991). *Beyond Mind Games.* Ithaca, N.Y.: American Demographics Books.

Pope John Paul II. (1993). *Veritatis Splendor.*

————. (1991). *Centesimus Annus.*

Roberts, Donald F., Foehr, Ulla, Rideout, Victoria, & Brodie, Mollyann. (1999). Kids and media at the new millennium: A Kaiser Family Foundation Report. San Francisco: Kaiser Family Foundation.

Rotstein, Gary. (1999). Final arrangements. *Pittsburgh Post Gazette,* May 23–25.

Savan, Leslie. (1994). *The Sponsored Life*. Philadelphia: Temple University Press.

Schafer, Sarah. (1997). Mourning becomes electric. *Inc.,* September 16.

Schall, Norman, Director of Catholic Cemeteries for the Diocese of Joliet. (2000). Telephone interview with Michael L. Budde, February 2.

Schindler, David L. (1996). *Heart of the World, Center of the Church*. Grand Rapids: Eerdmans.

Schor, Juliet. (1991). *The Overworked American*. New York: Basic Books.

Scott, James. (1985). *Weapons of the Weak: Everyday forms of Peasant Resistance*. New Haven: Yale University Press.

SCI/Service Corporation International. (1997). Press Release.

Shanahan, James, and Morgan, Michael. (1999). *Television and Its Viewers: Cultivation Theory and Research*. New York: Cambridge University Press.

Shindehette, Susan. (2000). Last embrace. *People,* January 24.

Shipp, Sigmund. (1996). The road not taken: Alternative strategies for black economic development in the United States. *Journal of Economic Issues, 30*.

Stackhouse, Max. (1991). John Paul on ethics and the "New Capitalism." *Christian Century,* May 29.

———. (1987). *Public Theology and Political Economy*. Grand Rapids: Eerdmans.

Stackhouse, Max, McCann, Dennis, & Roels, Shirley (Eds.). (1995). *On Moral Business*. Grand Rapids: Eerdmans.

Strate, Lance. (1991). The cultural meaning of beer commercials. *Advances in Consumer Research,* No. 18.

Strout, Erin. (1999). Digging up sales. *Sales and Marketing Management,* April.

Thavis, John. (1999). Good liturgy vs. good viewing: keeping the sacred in TV Masses. *Catholic News Service,* September 3.

USA Today. (1997). Chaplains-for-hire provide services in workplace. November 14.

U.S. Catholic. (1994). Sharing the faith: helping young people to lead moral lives. February.

Veash, Nicole. (2000). Church floats charity on Rio stock exchange. *Daily Telegraph,* September 10.

Verbeke, William. (1992). Advertisers do not persuade customers: they create societies around their brands to maintain power in the marketplace. *International Journal of Advertising.* 16:1.

Verberg, Peter. (1998). Will Loewen be buried? *Canadian Business,* September 25.

Waide, John. (1987). The making of self and world in advertising. *Journal of Business Ethics,* No. 6.

Wasielewski, Henry. (n.d.) Personal documentary archive at www.xroads.com/~funerals/.

Werner, Ben. (1999). State scrutinizes pre-pay funeral deals. *Baltimore Business Journal,* April 16.

Welles, Edward. (1997). Chaplain to the new economy. *Inc,* November.

Whyte, William F. (1999). The Mondragon cooperatives in 1976 and 1998. *Industrial and Labor Relations Review.* 52(3).

Williams, Oliver F. & Houck, John W. (1992). *Catholic Thought and the New World Order.* Notre Dame, Ind.: University of Notre Dame Press.

Willmott, H. (1993). Strength is ignorance, slavery is freedom: managing culture in modern organizations. *Journal of Management Studies.* 30(4).

Wirpsa, Leslie. (1998). Death care giants team up with church. *National Catholic Reporter,* January 30.

———. (1998). Funeral giants, church make two new deals. *National Catholic Reporter,* April 10.

Woodstock Business Conference. (n.d.) Materials at www.georgetown.edu/centers/woodstock.

Worklife Report. (1999). Vol. 12, No. 1.

Wright, N. T. (1996). *Jesus and the Victory of God.* Minneapolis, Minn.: Fortress Press.

Index